Environment and Diplomacy in the Americas

Environment and Diplomacy in the Americas

edited by
Heraldo Muñoz

foreword by
Joao Baena Soares

Lynne Rienner Publishers ▪ Boulder & London

9-29-95

Published in the United States of America in 1992 by
Lynne Rienner Publishers, Inc.
1800 30th Street, Boulder, Colorado 80301

and in the United Kingdom by
Lynne Rienner Publishers, Inc.
3 Henrietta Street, Covent Garden, London WC2E 8LU

Published with the General Secretariat and the Committee on the Environment of the
Permanent Council, Organization of American States

Library of Congress Cataloging-in-Publication Data
Environment and diplomacy in the Americas / edited by Heraldo Muñoz.
    p.   cm.
    Includes bibliographical references.
    Contents: The environment in inter-American relations / Heraldo Muñoz—
Statement by the Hon. José Lutzenberger, minister of the environment of Brazil, to
the Working Group of the Environment, Permanent Council of the OAS—Statement
by the Hon. Luis Alvarado, minister of national assets of Chile and president of the
National Committee on the Environment, to the Working Group of the Environment,
Permanent Council of the OAS—A commitment to life : Statement by Dr. Mostafa K.
Tolba, executive director of the United Nations Environment Program to the Seventh
Ministerial Meeting of the Latin American and Caribbean Region—Inter-American
Program of Action for Environmental Protection / Organization of American States—
Annexes. Selected documents on environment and development of Latin America and
the Caribbean. Selected United Nations documents on environment and development.
    ISBN 1-55587-390-1
    1. Environmental policy—Latin America. 2. Environmental protection—Latin
America—International cooperation. 3. Latin America—Economic conditions—1982-
4. Latin America—Foreign relations—United States. 5. United States—Foreign
relations—Latin America. I. Muñoz, Heraldo.
HC130.E5E59 1992
363.7'056'098—dc20
                            92-4480
                            CIP

British Cataloguing in Publication Data
A Cataloguing in Publication record for this book
is available from the British Library.

Printed and bound in the United States of America

Contents

Foreword

JOAO BAENA SOARES

The Organization of American States has recently strengthened its institutional framework to deal with environmental issues, which have long been on its agenda. The OAS General Assembly, meeting in Santiago, Chile, in June 1991, adopted an "Inter-American Program of Action for Environmental Protection," and instructed the Permanent Council to establish a Standing Committee through which the Organization's environmental policy should be proposed, and measures for regional cooperation developed, coordinated, evaluated, and monitored.

The Inter-American Program intends "to use the OAS as a forum for a rational, constructive, hemisphere-wide debate, free of recrimination, aimed at developing a specific regional approach in order to contribute to implementation of the proposals of global scope that environmental protection requires."

As the natural forum for this inter-American dialogue, the OAS is the appropriate channel for a debate conducive to establishing an environmental cooperation policy for the Americas. There is ample space as well as dire need for consultation and negotiation on issues related to the environment.

Today, democratic governments rule almost all of the nations of the hemisphere. Strengthening of democracy in the Americas has greatly improved the possibilities for hemispheric understanding and cooperation. It is a timely occasion to launch the Inter-American Program of Action on Environmental Protection.

Member-states bring to the OAS the richness and diversity of natural resources that characterize the Americas. Each nation faces its own unique development and environment problems; all nations face together the need to ensure that their development styles are compatible with environmental protection.

Every state has a sovereign right to use its environment for developmental purposes. There is also a basic need to protect the environment, in order to grant the people their right to live in a healthy and adequate milieu. The need to use natural resources as a fundamental ingredient for economic growth and integral development competes with the necessity to prevent environmental degradation. Competition between those two requirements poses a number of policy alternatives both at the national and international levels. However, competition does not necessarily imply conflict. Natural resources should be exploited only in harmony with the environment.

Latin America and the Caribbean are richly endowed with natural resources, which have been a traditional basis of their development: land under cultivation—less than one-fourth of arable land of the region—is almost 12 percent of the world's total; nearly one-fourth of potentially arable land, one-fifth of hydroelectric resources, and 46 percent of tropical forests lie in Latin America and the Caribbean. They are important producers and exporters of food, oil, coal, and minerals. Manufacturing, which is currently the leading contributor to GDP, was developed largely upon the natural resources base.

Latin America and the Caribbean have the right and the need to develop. There is a large—and broadening—gap in income between developing countries of the region and their neighbors to the north, as illustrated by the fact that in 1989 median GNP per capita amounted to US$1,760 for Latin American and Caribbean countries, compared to averages of US$19,030 in Canada, and US$20,910 in the United States.

Unequal income distribution and widespread poverty have long been the most serious problems in Latin America and the Caribbean. Today, two out of every five people in the region live below poverty lines. Beyond their economic implications and their reflection of social injustice, inequality and destitution pose serious threats to democratic stability and consolidation. Development is needed to correct social imbalance, and to improve standards of living in Latin America and the Caribbean.

After a decade of profound financial, economic, and social crisis, governments of the region have undertaken sweeping structural adjustments to resume development and growth. Considerations related to the protection of the environment have been incorporated into the new development policies. The priority assigned to sustainable development is a welcome approach to a problem that did not receive sufficient attention in the past. Natural resources have been depleted in many cases to feed the need for economic growth. Urbanization has frequently followed ecologically harmful patterns.

Countries of the region have traditionally suffered serious deterioration of their environments. Rules and practices of the global economic system have been a contributing factor. Developing countries of the hemisphere have confronted the need to use their natural resources in an indiscriminate manner in order to adapt to the demand of developed countries for raw materials and primary goods, which have historically been their main exports. Not enough weight is usually given to the direct relationship that frequently exists between industrial countries' policies and environmental deterioration in Latin American and the Caribbean. Countries of the South have been subject to negative consequences on their environment flowing from development styles in the North. Domestic demand, affected by skewed income distribution, and imitation of foreign patterns, has added to the pressure in this respect. Poverty itself, forcing people to exploit nature without regard for the consequences, has also been a source of degradation.

Recent accords on nuclear arms limitation are a welcome development for the safety of mankind: they might prevent the worst tragedy in history, nuclear winter. However, nuclear arsenals, atomic reactors, wastes that have been dumped in the oceans, submarines and space artifacts, and uninterrupted experimentation still loom as momentous threats.

The so-called greenhouse effect, caused by emissions of carbon dioxide and other gases, is another serious menace to the quality of life. Carbon dioxide from deforestation in Latin America and the Caribbean is about 40 percent of the world total. However, deforestation contributes only about 14 percent to global warming, whose main source is emission of gases from industry. Carbon dioxide industrial emission is highly concentrated in developed countries, which account for about 75 percent of total emissions. Destruction of the ozone layer in the atmosphere is an important concern, since it affects human health as well as several marine species and plants.

Developed and developing countries thus confront common challenges that can best be met through concerted action. Each American state should decide on the use of its own natural resources. International cooperation, however, should be helpful in ensuring environmental protection, insofar as it is based on mutually discussed and freely accepted proposals for cooperative undertakings in this field.

Beyond the need to agree on ways to promote environmental conservation, the countries of the Americas are also aware of opportunities they have to join in contributing to the preservation of some valuable, scarce resources that will enhance quality of life in the hemisphere and the world. The use of resources of the Antarctic, a continent having a unique ecology whose value to the rest of the world is still being probed, and utilization of outer space for communication purposes are two examples.

Environment and Diplomacy in the Americas presents to an interested audience a selection of testimonies on the problems affecting conservation of the environment, and suggested responses to such questions.

Ambassador Heraldo Muñoz, Permanent Representative of Chile to the OAS, and Chairman of the Permanent Council's Committee on the Environment, had the excellent idea of publishing this book, and has been the driving force for this publication. Other distinguished contributors include the Honorable José Lutzenberger, Minister of the Environment of Brazil; the Honorable Luis Alvarado, Minister of National Assets of Chile; and Dr. Mostafa K. Tolba, Executive Director of the United Nations Environment Program.

The book is also intended to disseminate the contents of the main official inter-American and international documents that have been adopted as the basis for action at a time when there is increasing consciousness of the need to ensure that use of natural resources for development be consistent with preservation of environmental integrity.

We trust that *Environment and Diplomacy in the Americas* will be useful for those people and institutions directly involved in its subject matter. We are also confident that it will appeal to the general public. Protection of the environment requires an active participation of government officials and diplomats. It also calls, however, for universal awareness that individual care for the common patrimony of natural surroundings is fundamental to avoiding its degradation.

To the extent that this book stimulates inter-American cooperation on ecological matters, and provokes people to act in a manner compatible with conservation of the environment, it will have accomplished its main objective.

The Environment in Inter-American Relations

HERALDO MUNOZ

For a long time the subject of the environment was absent from the foreign policy priorities of the countries of the hemisphere, and therefore from the agenda of the inter-American system as well, except for isolated instances such as the 1940 Western Hemisphere Convention for the Protection of Nature and Conservation of Flora, Fauna, and Natural Beauties of the Countries of America. However, this lack of interest, which was not only regional but worldwide, began to change in the early 1970s as the result of debate that culminated in the United Nations conference on the human environment held in Stockholm in 1972.

Notable change has occurred since then. The subject of the environment is now a political priority in the foreign policies of most countries. The Paris meeting of the Group of Seven highly developed countries (G7) in 1989 was dubbed the "green summit" precisely because of the importance it afforded discussions of world environmental problems. This concern was also evident at the Houston G7 meeting in mid-July 1990, when the final communiqué cited as one of its most important responsibilities "providing future generations with an environment the health, beauty and economic potential of which were not threatened."[1]

This change in attitude is in part attributable to nongovernmental ecology organizations and the Green Parties of the United States and Western Europe. Their activism contributed to elevating the importance of environmental issues in the foreign policy agenda of those countries. One result has been the growing significance of environmental matters in Washington's relations with Latin America and the Caribbean as the 1990s begin.

As in the rest of the world, concern for the environment has rapidly been acquiring greater importance in Latin America and the Caribbean. In contrast with a few years ago, today there are many nongovernmental groups dedicated to the study and promotion of environmental conservation. And public opinion polls demonstrate that Latin Americans assign great importance to the control of environmental pollution in their large cities, to the contamination of coastal areas, and, in general, to the deterioration of ecosystems. At the government level, too, increasing urgency is being given to environmental problems. In fact, such countries as Colombia, Venezuela, Peru, Brazil, Mexico, Ecuador, Bolivia, Costa Rica, and Chile, among others, have recently approved environmental protection codes or created national commissions or ministries of the environment to formulate and apply environmental protection policies.

The different mechanisms of consultation and cooperation in Latin America and the Caribbean have also served to stimulate advances in the discussion of the region's environmental protection policies and to limit, neutralize, or reverse processes that degrade local, regional, or world ecological balances. The environment has become a permanent agenda item for the Rio Group during its meetings. In the final communiqué of the meeting held by the Rio Group in Caracas, October 1990, the presidents of the Rio Group countries committed themselves to "maintain constant coordination in multi-lateral fora on the environment in order to harmonize our positions and assure them more efficiency."[2] Similar concern is shown by the countries grouped into the Amazon Pact, CARICOM, and the recently created Central American Commission on the Environment and Development.

At the regional level, significant progress has occurred in the preparation of diagnosis and action program proposals to confront the hemisphere's environmental problems. Outstanding environmental policy efforts have been carried out in Latin America and the Caribbean by the United Nations Environment Programme (UNEP), which agreed to a "call to action" at its Seventh Ministerial-Level Regional Meeting in Trinidad-Tobago in October 1990; by the Latin American and Caribbean Commission on Development and the Environment, established in 1989 with the support of the Inter-American Development Bank (IDB) and the United Nations Development Programme (UNDP), which produced the report known as *Our Own Agenda*; by ECLAC, which organized a meeting that led to the adoption of the Tlatelolco Platform on the Environment and Development; and, at the hemispheric level, by the Working Group on Environmental Protection of the Permanent Council of the Organization of American States (OAS), which produced the Inter-American Program of Action on the Environment. All these efforts to a greater or lesser extent constitute preparatory steps for the United Nations Conference on the Environment and Development, to be held in Rio de Janeiro in 1992.

It is clear that as we begin the 1990s the deterioration of the environment is a problem of the highest political urgency, and tied to the systematic development of the Americas. Protection of the environment has been transformed into a development priority for hemisphere countries, and into a matter that also concerns their security.

THE ENVIRONMENT AND SECURITY

In its broadest sense, the concept of "security" refers to the situation in which a person, institution, or country is free from any danger, damage, or threat. Traditionally, Latin American and Caribbean countries defined their security in terms of the classical notions of national sovereignty and military defense of territorial integrity. From this conventional perspective, security ultimately depends on the arms and adequately trained personnel available to meet foreign and domestic threats.

However, this way of conceiving security appears to be insufficient for responding to a series of risks and threats of a nonmilitary nature that Latin American and Caribbean nations face. A reformulation debate has given rise to new approaches to the concept of security: Since the end of the 1970s "collective economic security" has been on the regional agenda. This revised notion of security includes those conditions that increase or diminish the capacity of individual countries to resolve critical social and economic problems and to achieve a more equitable and democratic internal order. The relationship of these conditions to the security of each individual country is evident. The accumulation of tensions and unsatisfied demands, and foreign restraints that obstruct, impede, or block internal development all represent situations at least as dangerous as military threats.

The security of a country cannot be dependent solely upon tanks and bombers. A nation's security also depends on its climate, the quality and availability of land for cultivation, its water and marine resources, the normal functioning of its water basins, its genetic resources, and the diversity of its wildlife. And so, the incorporation of environmental issues into security approaches in the region has become necessary.[3] If a nation is denied the environmental factors it needs for normal development there is no doubt that its economy, at the very least, will be affected. Taking the situation to the extreme, the social and political structure of that nation may be seriously damaged, possibly to the point of provoking its disintegration.[4]

The international dimension of the environmental problem and its impact on security results from the fact that much of the aggression the environment now suffers has effects that go beyond the borders of the country where the abuse occurs. The attempts by some developed countries to export toxic and radioactive waste to countries in Latin America, and, in general, the interest in relocating in the South some industrial plants that produce environmental impacts unacceptable to the developed countries are examples of the nonmilitary aggression to which the regional environment is being exposed.

Some environmental aggression is clearly worldwide. That is the case, for example, with global warming (the greenhouse effect), the destruction of the ozone layer, the loss of biodiversity (accelerated destruction of species), and the contamination of oceans. Other environmental problems are more regional in their scope, such as the deterioration of the water basins and ecosystems shared by various countries in Central and South America. For example, deforestation and misuse of the land in the higher elevations of the basins fill the rivers with large quantities of sediment downstream that may eventually be deposited in and obstruct navigational channels in other countries.

Since the seriousness of the damage caused to nature puts world security and the future of humanity at risk, the logical way to confront the situation is cooperatively to search for collective solutions and to support national efforts. As the Latin American and Caribbean Commission on Development and the Environment states in the document, *Our Own Agenda*, "There is no room for doubt that the most sensible course is to build the foundation of a pact for survival. That foundation will be solid to the extent that we can work together. Let us take a step forward together and let us call on those to negotiate who have the will to act generously, vision and a sense of solidarity with the future of human civilization."[5]

THE END OF THE COLD WAR AND THE ENVIRONMENT IN INTER-AMERICAN RELATIONS

With the end of the Cold War and the changes that have taken place in the former Socialist world, the organizing principle of US post-war foreign policy—the containment of the Soviet Union and of Communism—has, in practical terms, ceased to exist. The principal threat to the United States has disappeared, and along with it the perspectives through which Washington viewed the world and built alliances and regional understandings of both diplomatic and military nature. And of course changes in hemispheric relations have unfolded as of the moment in which one of the principal factors which provoked the decline of the inter-American system ceased to exist: that is, the perception that the inter-American system was merely an instrument in the context of the East-West confrontation.

In the United States, while most leaders agree that the Cold War has ended, there is as yet no consensus around any new national thesis. That means there is a conceptual vacuum in foreign policy, although a relative decline is perceived in military concerns in favor of economic matters. Many issues have emerged to compete for the designation of new national security priority. According to Theodore Sorensen, the temptation is to include each leader's favorite topic as the basis for a new US security paradigm.[6] As a matter of fact, the deterioration of the environment, along with other themes such as drug-trafficking, illegal migration, economic competition, and the promotion of democracy, is one of the themes being emphasized among the new security priorities in the post-Cold War era.

However, if the ecological question is unilaterally defined as a matter vital to the United States' national security and to relations between Washington and Latin America, there exists the danger of transferring the traditional tensions and distrust of inter-American relations to the subject of the environment (as has already partly occurred in the case of drug-trafficking). Disagreements and fears could become even stronger considering the fact that in the emerging new world context, without the ideological underpinnings of the Cold War, the logic of power politics would take on greater vigor, accentuating the asymmetries in the treatment of hemispheric affairs.

The challenge before the Latin American and Caribbean countries is to see to it that environmental issues in inter-American relations are approached from a new perspective. Emphasis must be placed on the practical necessity of defining and treating environmental issues in light of common security, which requires the perspective of international cooperation and coordinated actions among all the countries of the hemisphere, excluding unilateral actions, and in accordance with a general criterion of solidarity.

ENVIRONMENTAL COOPERATION
VS. NATIONAL SOVEREIGNTY

One principal difficulty in discussing the environment within the hemisphere has been how to confront such problems as contamination and environmental deterioration, which have neither national nor ideological boundaries, while at the same time preserving national sovereignty and the basic principles of inter-American law, including the principle of nonintervention.

We must accept the premise that, while all countries contaminate, it is possible to distinguish degrees of responsibility that each State has for degradation of the planet. Advances in this direction, however, have been problematic. It sometimes seems to developed countries that the developing countries are most responsible for damage to the environment—one example is the public concern often voiced in the developed nations for the deforestation of the Amazon basin.

However, if we consider two areas that excite more attention from the international community—the destruction of the ozone layer and the greenhouse effect—scientific research shows a different panorama. In the first case, the contribution of Latin America and the Caribbean to the production and utilization of gases that degrade stratospheric ozone (principally chloroflourocarbons and halogens) is infinitesimal. The study, *Chile: Strategy on Ozone Layer Protection* estimates that all of Latin American and the Caribbean represent only 3 percent of world usage of chloroflourocarbons; North America alone consumes 35 percent; and the United States, the former Soviet Union, and the rest of the industrialized countries, including Eastern Europe, produce 95 percent of those gases.[7] Something similar occurs in the case of global warming. It is calculated that carbonic anhydride generated in industrial processes, the burning of fossil fuels, and deforestation represent 50 percent of all the greenhouse effect gases emitted into the atmosphere. Some estimates put the share of Latin America and the Caribbean between 12.9 percent and 14.4 percent of total world emissions of carbonic anhydride.[8]

From the Latin American perspective, attention must be paid to the environmental damage caused by overconsumption in rich countries. This thesis is supported by studies that demonstrate that such phenomena as global warming are due more to the excessive use of hydrocarbons in industrialized countries than to the destruction of rain forests in the Amazon. There are also examples of how certain consumption habits in developed nations generate demand for products that result in environmental damage or the depletion of natural resources in Latin America and the Caribbean.[9] These perspectives have in the past led some political sectors in the less-developed countries to take some extreme positions—for example, that environmental concerns in industrialized countries were in fact a hypocritical attempt to deny economic growth to poor countries, in order to conserve their natural beauties for the sake of developed countries' ecotourism.

Fortunately, the most acute stage of the controversy between international action on the environment and national sovereignty has now passed. Although the countries of Latin America and the Caribbean have not accepted a concept of limited sovereignty, they have expressed that sovereignty must not constitute an obstacle to the negotiation of just and balanced agreements, in which the duties and the rights of the parties are clearly defined. The Declaration of Brasilia, signed by the states of Latin America and the Caribbean, reaffirms that "each State has the sovereign right to freely administer its natural resources," but immediately adds that such right does "not exclude, but on the contrary, reinforces, the necessity of international cooperation."[10]

In summary, the Latin American and Caribbean countries have accepted that States have the sovereign right to exploit their resources in accordance with their own environmental policies and development strategies, but, by the same token, accepting the necessity to cooperate, they have the duty to prevent, reduce, or avoid all adverse effects or prejudices to the environment under their control as well as to that of other States or zones outside their national jurisdiction.

DEVELOPMENT, THE ENVIRONMENT AND THE DOUBLE-DETERIORATION PARADOX

Another complicating factor of the debate on international aspects of the environment that inevitably affects hemisphere relations is the link between environmental protection and socioeconomic development.

Although they recognize the link between environmental matters and development, the United States and other developed countries often tend to associate the deterioration of ecosystems with pressures derived from high demographic growth. According to this thesis, population growth in developing countries exceeds the overload capacity of the ecosystems, thus contributing to the deterioration of the environment.

Clearly there is a relationship between population density and environmental quality, but that relationship is strongly mediated by the model or style of development. If that model generates impoverishment, heavy migration from rural areas to urban centers, pressures on land use that result in its overutilization, and the extractive exploitation of natural resources, it eventually provokes, as we see in Latin America and the Caribbean, extreme deterioration of the environment. Still, from the perspective of developing countries, the pressure exerted on the environment by the inhabitants of an industrialized, high-consumption country is notably more harmful than that exerted by the inhabitants of a poor country. However, there now seems to be a growing consensus that environmental decay is linked to both the excesses of prosperity and the conditions of poverty, and that both conditions have in common a style of development that assumes natural capital is infinite.[11]

From the Latin American viewpoint, it is also difficult to advance toward the creation of conditions for effective environmental protection and conservation so long as there is the heavy burden of servicing foreign debt, the fluctuations of world trade, and the internal economic adjustment processes that are being carried out.[12] The governments of the region have repeatedly argued that key elements in any approach to conserve hemisphere ecosystems are to address the conditions of underdevelopment and poverty, alleviate the weight of external debt, and favor the achievement of more equitable international economic conditions.

There is a growing commitment in Latin America and the Caribbean to a development model based on the rational utilization of natural resources and on the necessity for adopting measures designed to limit or reverse processes that degrade local, regional, or world ecological balance. But it is considered difficult to produce substantive progress without greater international cooperation. As the Rio Group said at the Caracas meeting in October 1990, "The possibility for our countries to assume concrete commitments and participate effectively in international instruments, programs and projects in the field of environmental protection depends, to a large extent, on our having adequate technology on accessible terms and additional financial resources."[13] Cooperation for environmental conservation must also include the promotion of pure and applied scientific research, including access to scientific information; and the transfer to developing countries, under favorable conditions, of technologies that are clean and designed for environmental conservation and for the enhancement of national decisionmaking processes related to environmental matters.

Addressing the issue of technology transfer in the agenda of inter-American relations is a challenge for the countries of the region. Differences on the subject are well-known. In fact, recent years have witnessed tension and disagreement between the White House and several Latin American governments attributable to the importance with which the United States imbues the protection of intellectual property. The pressures exerted on Latin American countries to change their respective legislations to protect pharmaceutical patents is one case in point. It is highly likely that this area of conflict will broaden now that, in the era of biotechnology and microelectronics, the protection of intellectual property represents much more significant benefits for the private sector than those earned through the technological innovation that ushered in the famous "green revolution" of the 1970s.

Furthermore, it could be argued that Latin American countries suffer a double-deterioration paradox. In the first place, they are the victims of major environmental problems, such as global warming and the deterioration of the ozone layer, which are mainly caused by the developed countries; and, second, in order to contribute to solving those environmental problems originating principally in the developed world, they must borrow scarce financial resources or purchase high-priced technologies, consequently adding damage to their national budgets and development strategies.

The high cost of technology protected by intellectual property rights does not adequately reflect the contribution of the biodiversity found principally in the less-developed countries. As one source reminds us, "half of all prescriptions dispensed in the world have their origins in wild organisms. In the United States, the value of these medicines and drugs amounts to some US$14 billion a year . . . [but] the wild genetic material is found mostly in the tropical South."[14] Similarly, there are more species of birds in the Sangay National park in Ecuador than in all of North America, while the Choco region in Colombia has potentially more plant species than all of those that have been conserved in the history of the United States.[15]

Latin American countries are also concerned with what they perceive as a growing tendency in Washington to use environmental protection to impose nontariff barriers on exports from developing countries, with resulting distortions of international trade and the provisions of GATT Article 20. Latin American countries question this kind of attitude particularly when it comes from sectors that did not show much environmental consciousness in the past, and because it disregards the progress made by producers, particularly in the private sector, in environmental protection. The Latin American productive sectors have come to understand the necessity of incorporating environmental parameters in their costs of production so as to remain competitive in the export market since, according to one source, "very soon the international market will simply not accept products that are not environmentally safe."[16]

ROUTES TO THE FUTURE

There is the risk that the subject of the environment will be transformed into another point of misunderstanding between the United States and Latin America. Inter-American conflict over this matter will tend to increase to the extent that the United States (or any other country) unilaterally defines environmental protection as a problem exclusively of its external security, thus dismissing real dialogue, cooperative efforts, and solidarity on the regional and world level. Without concrete expressions of cooperation, confrontation will be unavoidable.

But there are various areas of inter-American affairs where cooperation is possible. Such areas include:

1. implementing programs to promote environmental consciousness as an omnipresent dimension of education;
2. promoting the transfer of clean technologies and those that favor protection and conservation;
3. developing uniform terminology and common criteria for the protection of natural resources and biodiversity;
4. harmonizing environmental legislation among the States of the hemisphere;
5. promoting studies to review national accounts to incorporate the impact of natural resource use;
6. developing regional policies on prevention of environmental accidents and the elimination of radioactive, toxic, and dangerous wastes in accordance with pertinent international juridical instruments; and
7. promoting and supporting the training of human resources in environmental matters.

One interesting, although modest, step in hemisphere environmental cooperation is the Enterprise for the Americas Initiative announced by President Bush in June 1990. It provides for the exchange of foreign debt for environmental protection projects. Although Washington never explicitly recognized a linkage between foreign debt and conservation of the environment, it has done so indirectly by introducing the "swap" mechanism as part of the initiative.

Part of the legislation related to the Enterprise for the Americas Initiative has already been approved under the Agriculture Law of 1990. The law provides for the reduction of concessional agriculture debt, allowing interest on such credits to be paid in local currency, and designating that money to a fund for environmental protection. The law also authorizes the president of the United States to sign bilateral agreements with beneficiary countries that want to make use of that facility. Each country will have to establish an Enterprise for the Americas Initiative Environmental Protection Fund to be administered by a committee made up of:

1. one or more representatives named by the president of the United States,
2. one or more representatives designated by the beneficiary country, and
3. representatives of local nongovernmental organizations dedicated to environmental issues.

The types of projects to be financed fall into nine categories, from the restoration, protection, or sustainable use of the oceans and the atmosphere, to the promotion of regenerative methodologies in agriculture, fishing, use of waters, and forestry. Finally, the same legislation creates, in the United States, an "Environment for the Americas Board" to advise the president on the subject and supervise the activities of the national committees.

Perhaps one of the most important efforts being undertaken to promote inter-American cooperation for environmental conservation is the Inter-American Action Program for Environmental Protection approved by the General Assembly of the OAS in Santiago, Chile, in June 1991. The program contains two chapters that enumerate action measures to be implemented by individual member States and action measures to be promoted through a regional cooperative effort. In addition, the program provides for the adoption of institutional mechanisms to coordinate and evaluate the action measures, and creates a permanent commission on the environment.

Obviously, technical cooperation plus the relevant aspects of the Enterprise for the Americas Initiative are not by themselves sufficient to meet the problem of environmental deterioration. It would be an error to think of "depoliticizing" the subject and to adopt a merely technical approach. The central thrust of the inter-American perspective must be political and, in the ultimate analysis, must lead to the promotion of a hemispheric debate, without recriminations, oriented to the formulation of a just, common, specifically hemispheric-focused design to contribute to the worldwide task of environmental protection.

NOTES

I am grateful for the support provided by Daniel Asenjo in the research of this paper. This article reflects only the views of the author and not necessarily those of the Committee on the Environment of the OAS, over which he presides, or those of the government of Chile.

1. "Reunión Cumbre declara máxima prioridad de conversaciones sobre Medio Ambiente." *Official Text*, Information Service (Embassy of the United States: Chile, 13 July 1990), 14.

2. Grupo de Río, "Declaración de Caracas," 12 October 1990.

3. On the evolution of this new approach to security in Latin America and in particular the incorporation of the ecology dimension therein, see the publications of the South American Peace Commission. Specifically, South American Peace Commission, *Principios de la Seguridad Democrática Regional*, ILET, July 1988; Manuel Baquedano, *La Seguridad Ecológica en América del Sur*, Study Document Series, No. 3, South American Peace Commission; Raul Brañes, *Seguridad Ambiental en América del Sur: Los principales problemas y los nuevos desafíos de la soberanía*, Working Document Series, No. 5, South American Peace Commission; and Juan Somavía and José Miguel Insulza (eds.), *Seguridad Democrática Regional, Una Concepción Alternativa* (Caracas: Editorial Nueva Sociedad, 1990).

4. Vicente Sánchez, "Modalidades de desarrollo, relaciones internacionales y políticas ambientales" paper presented to the Primer Seminario Latinoamericano de Sistemas Ambientales para la Planificación (UNAM: Mexico City, 2–5 December 1985).

5. Latin American and Caribbean Commission on Development and the Environment, *Our Own Agenda* (IDB-PNUD, 1990), 41.

6. Theodore Sorensen, *Foreign Affairs* (Summer 1990), 3.

7. Ozone Team Manager, *Chile: Strategy on Ozone Layer Protection* (Santiago: Ñielol, 1991), 14.

8. *Our Own Agenda*, op. cit., 41 et seq.

9. Vicente Sánchez, op. cit.

10. "Declaración de Brasilia," VI Reunión Ministerial sobre el Medio Ambiente en América Latina y el Caribe, 30–31 March 1989.

11. See CEPAL, *El Desarrollo Sustentable: Transformación Productiva, Equidad y Medio Ambiente* (United Nations, January 1991), 9.

12. The argument has been advanced that service on their foreign debt has forced debtor countries to overexploit their natural resources for export with consequent damage to the environment. However, that argument has been questioned by Steven Sanderson, who has shown that for Latin America as a whole, agricultural, forestry, and fishing exports have exceeded the levels before the debt crisis on only one occasion between 1980 and 1990 and that, additionally, the last two decades witnessed a decline in the importance of the raw materials producer and exporter sectors, even during the debt crisis period of the 1980s. See Steven Sanderson, "Policies Without Politics: Environmental Affairs

in OECD Latin American Relations in the 1990's," mimeo, (University of Florida, April 1990).

13. Declaración de Caracas, op. cit.

14. *Our Common Future: The World Commission on Environment and Development* (Washington, D.C.: Earthcan Books, 1987), 155–156.

15. Roberto Guimarães, "La Ecopolítica del Desarrollo Sustentable" in Roberto Russell (ed.) *La Agenda Internacional en los Años 90* (Buenos Aires: GEL-RIAL, 1990), 75.

16. Eberhard Meller, Environmental Policy Director of the Federation of German Industries, *El Diario* (Santiago 14 March 1991), 24.

Environment and Development: A View from Brazil

JOSE LUTZENBERGER

At a dinner given by President Collor of Brazil to honor Rodrigo Borja Cevallos, president of Ecuador, both the host and President Borja made statements that struck me as exceedingly important. The two presidents agreed that what we need in Latin America today is development—heightened development—to resolve our problems of social injustice and inequity, but that we must redefine what we understand as progress or development. Because if development means extending to the entire planet the things we seek today—e.g., the quality of life in this country, and in countries such as Germany, France, Switzerland, the Netherlands—that is just plain suicide. It has no future; it just cannot be.

Our planet cannot support a consumer society with the excessive use of commodities to which we are accustomed in the United States. It would be impossible to extend them to the entire planet. Suffice it to consider a very simple extrapolation: in the United States we have one automobile for every 1.7 inhabitants. The planet already has 500 million cars for a population of 5.4 billion. If we were to extend this type of development to the entire planet, we would end up with some 3 billion automobiles. That is out of the question; the atmosphere cannot stand it.

So we must rethink our goals. And the first ones that must redesign their economic model are the countries of the First World. All of us must do some rethinking—but they even more than we, because they are the ones responsible for the major environmental problems, such as the deteriorating atmosphere and world climate.

The concern that is troubling even the United Nations today—the "greenhouse effect"—is only one of the areas in which the aggression and interference with natural processes, perpetrated by modern industrial society, have reached global levels.

The situation is in fact much more serious than we think. Everyone should be now be familiar with the discussion of the "greenhouse effect." Its most salient feature is a concern with linear extrapolation over the next 50 or 100 years. We are told that as carbon dioxide (along with other gases, such as methane and other contributors to the greenhouse effect) is released into the atmosphere, there will be a slow but progressive rise in the temperature of the planet, which—perhaps by the year 2050 or 2080—will result in serious climatic upsets. Europe's temperate climate will become subtropical. The polar caps may melt. Sea levels will rise four meters.

These dangers thus loom forty, fifty, or one hundred years down the road. Obviously most politicians (as well as technocrats) operate in a limited time frame, generally bounded by the date of the next election. By the time they have amassed a certain amount of power, they have also reached a certain age with an implicit short-term outlook; this is an accepted fact that does not bother many people.

But anyone who is familiar with vital processes and has a holistic or ecological view of nature realizes that when we have to cope with such complex systems as human life or the planet's climate system, there is no way of drawing open-ended linear extrapolations.

A human being can take a lot of abuse, withstanding violent aggression up to a certain point and then collapsing. Consider the following hypothesis: let us assume that I am a little dwarf who is forever pushing against an object. I keep pushing, time after time, and nothing happens. Past experience tells me that I can continue to push indefinitely to no avail. There is a point where knowledge provides no further assistance.

Vital processes are like that: they will take a lot of punishment up to a certain point, after which there is a quick reversal. By that time, it is too late to be sorry; and no additional information will help.

A dangerous attitude prevails today. A case in point is the White House conference on climate held early in 1990, at which the US government insisted upon more information and more research. That is a dangerous attitude. By now we have a hundred times the information necessary to spark a change in our position. If we are not making changes, it is because we do not want to.

Of course more research is needed. Research is good; it is important. But the knowledge we now possess suffices to tell us that modern industrial society is on a suicide course. Either we use the knowledge we already have to make the necessary decisions that, over time, will produce the necessary changes to ward off the disasters that are imminent, or our children will assuredly and in the near future have reason to curse us.

In my opinion, we should be guided by the basic precepts of wisdom. That is not happening. If I am performing an experiment, knowing that a possible failure will have unacceptable and irreversible results, I have no right to perform that experiment. That, however, is the type of experiment mankind is engaged in today. We are releasing into the atmosphere ever greater amounts of substances that will very soon trigger dramatic changes. And anyone observing events today can see that draconian changes are already taking place. Before we reach the point of no return, there is an interval where things hang in the balance long enough to give us a chance to pull back.

Over the past ten years, the entire planet has witnessed increasingly severe climatic changes. Recently I visited Rio Grande do Sul, the place where I was born, in southern Brazil. The past ten years have seen a series of floods and droughts in Rio Grande do Sul. It once had a subtropical, rainy, and very stable climate. Now its climate gets worse with each passing year. During my visit, there was a downpour, the likes of which I had never seen before: 15 centimeters—not millimeters!—in less than an hour. A week later there was another storm with 20 centimeters of rainfall in less than an hour. Such things had never happened in the past.

There is no point in confining our thinking to long-term extrapolations of developments that may inconvenience our great-great-grandchildren. The road from here to there may well prove intolerable. If the erratic climate we have already witnessed—and I was here in North America, in 1988, and saw the wheat fields in Manitoba where mounds of dust were swirling through the farms—continues to worsen, we will soon no longer be able to count on crop yields. Today 5.3 to 5.4 billion people are living on this planet, and we have fewer than 100 days of reserves. If severe climatic changes continue in North America, those reserve stocks will quickly be depleted.

What good is clement weather or a nice day for the beach in Scotland going to do us if there is nothing left to eat? Tens of millions of the world's population are now dying every year from malnutrition and starvation. Tomorrow the mortality rate may be hundreds of millions. They certainly will not go without a fuss. There will be a big uproar. And in today's world where violent dictators are trying to produce atom bombs and lethal chemicals for biological warfare, there is no telling what will happen.

So we must act. This will require a whole new view of the cosmos. Today we, the modern world society, divide the world into two groups: the developed and the underdeveloped (we do not use that word, because it would be insulting; so we call them the "developing countries"). Our belief is that the whole world should reach the status of the United States. Germany and others have done so. As we have seen, however, that is impossible. We are going to have to revise our thinking, because that type of progress has no future. It even uses as a yardstick of progress such things as the gross national product, which simply tots up the volume of goods billed without considering the real cash impact of that cash flow; does it bring greater happiness for a larger number of people or not? When we demolish whole mountains in Brazil to export iron ore and aluminum at dirt-cheap prices, the only thing our gross national product has to show for it is the foreign exchange income from the sale of those commodities; nothing in our balance sheet offsets the loss of the ore extracted from the mountain. We are poorer now than we were before. No one is keeping books of that account. Any industrialist or businessman who adopted the type of bookkeeping used by governments today would be bankrupt before he realized it. So we really have to review the basic precepts of our entire economic thinking. Today we say that we are producing oil, but since when have we produced oil? We are extracting oil, and we think we are getting rich in the process. Am I richer when I withdraw money from my account at the bank and spend it? Am I making money? Of course not! Yes, we are going to have to take a closer look at a lot of things.

In Latin America—where, despite everything, we still possess vast lands and enormous resources—it is time to think again and avoid the mistakes that have been and continue to be committed in the regions that are said to be developed but which, from many standpoints, I would consider to be poorly developed.

There is no future in a situation such as the one existing in the Netherlands. The entire planet cannot possibly attain their quality of life—the level of development and the squandered resources that are feasible only because they are working with *our* resources, the ones we sell them at rock-bottom prices.

We have a new government in Brazil today, a government whose philosophy is unlike that of its predecessor and various previous administrations. While we once viewed a vast wet tropical forest such as the Amazon region as merely a resource to be consumed, today we take a different view. Yes, we want development, but it must be defined in sharply different terms: development not confined to cash flows and the sale of materials, but a process calling for greater social justice, enhancing the well-being of a greater number of people, and producing a situation which is truly sustainable—one which can be maintained indefinitely and improves the commonwealth instead of consuming the environment. Unfortunately, almost all of the technologies we apply today entail degradation and depletion of natural resources.

More than 15 years ago (I was an environmentalist at the time), we were fighting a large-scale lake desalinization project at Laguna, in the State of Santa Catarina. Its plan was to close off the lakes to prevent the inflow of salt water, because fresh water was needed at the time for a steel plant. But more than 10,000 local shrimp fishermen complained that their means of existence would be destroyed. At that point one of the technocrats argued in the State Parliament: "But we have to consume nature in order to make money." (In Portuguese, the words even rhyme.) He went on to ask: "What is it that you people want? We are going to make so much money that anyone who wants shrimp can afford to buy it."

If that represents our attitude, not a stone will be left standing. And when the last shrimp is gone, there will not be enough money to buy more; you may have all the money you want, but there will be no shrimp to sell.

We must reassess our attitudes. The present government of Brazil, for example, has completely changed its philosophy about the Amazon region. Today we want to preserve that area: it is important not only to us but, like all ecosystems, to the planet as well.

Present-day industrial society has an absurd view of things. It looks at the planet and all it sees is a storehouse of resources—raw material that is there to be used by our generation as quickly and efficiently as possible. We think that any of our whims entitles us to demolish mountains, forgetting that planet earth is a living system. Today we have a new concept of modern ecology, one based on hard and disciplined science: the Gaia concept, which views earth as a living being. In a living being or organism, the different organs cannot fight each other—they can only complement each other. My heart can only function within my body. If I cut it out, it becomes simply a piece of flesh that will rot, and the rest of my body will rot as well. Only when it is beating inside me does it have a reason for existing. We have to learn to view the planet earth once again as did the peoples that, in our arrogance based on ignorance, we termed primitive.

The Indians, the Buddhists, and the black tribes of Africa had that global, holistic, unitary view of earth and believed they were part of a larger organism. We today—that is, the modern industrialized society of which we are (or want to be) a part—see nothing but resources. At worst, we see a sort of spaceship with ourselves as passengers, able to consume all that fills the chests and cupboards. But the world is a living organism that does not carry passengers. My heart is not my passenger—it is an integral part of my being, and I am an integral part of it. The plant outside, which produces the oxygen I consume, is an external organ of mine and just as important to me as my internal organs. And I am just as important to that plant as it is to me, because I produce the carbon dioxide it needs to survive.

So the industrialized society of today's world must set its sights on a new concept, a holistic view of social justice and sustainability of our achievements. Here in the Americas, both North and South, with our vast stretches of land and—despite all the damage we have wrought—with our wealth of resources, I believe that we can take a different stand, avoid the mistakes made by the so-called First World, and embark on a quest for sustainability.

People who know nothing about ecology tend to think that ecologists espouse absolute noninterference. We must not touch forests, we cannot cut down trees, and we should not meddle with anything. That is not the case. What ecology teaches us is that we should use nature the way human beings have always used it—in a sustainable fashion and by living on the interest accrued on our capital, not consuming the principal.

Until recently in Rio Grande do Sul, we had two different ways of utilizing nature: one was sustainable, the other was not. I use the past tense advisedly, for the second method no longer exists. The sustainable way of utilizing our land was farming. The farmer lived on the proceeds of his stockraising. If he had a thousand head of cattle, he knew that he could not kill more than 100 to 150 every year. He lived on the interest from his capital, which is why farmers have continued to farm for almost 300 years and will be able to do so indefinitely if they like.

In Rio Grande do Sul, Santa Catarina, and Paraná, we had one of the planet's most fantastic woodlands, filled with araucaria evergreens. When I was a lad of 18, the forests were virtually untouched. Then the lumberjacks went into the woods—which they had not made and to whose existence they had contributed nothing—and demolished as much as they could. They sold the result at the lowest possible price, and that was the end of the forest. If the lumberjacks had treated the forest the way the farmers deal with their livestock, the result would have been very different. They would have realized that if the aim is to preserve that 200- or 500-year-old stand of pines, they could fell one out of every 500 trees a year and the forest would not be depleted—like some carefully managed forests in Finland and Germany that continue to flourish.

But we have used the forest with a prospector's mentality. The prospector enters a world that does not belong to him, takes what he can, tramples and ravages everything, and then goes off to seek another world.

Unfortunately, our modern industrialized society by and large uses the same approach, consuming everything we can as quickly as possible. There is no future in that. So I call on those of us in the Organization of American States to rethink what we consider to be development and progress.

If progress and development are understood as nothing but an increase in the gross national product, expressed in terms of cash flow alone, it simply means demolishing more mountains, building more dams, moving ever greater quantities of materials, and continuing our destruction of the bases of human life. That is not progress. Progress should mean heightened social justice, enhanced well-being for a larger number of individuals, increased sustainability, and greater integration of civilization with the majestic process of creation.

Note: This chapter was delivered in a slightly different form as an address by José Lutzenberger, Brazil's minister of the environment, to the special working group on environmental protection of the OAS at its November 15, 1990, meeting.

Environment and Development:
A View From Chile

LUIS ALVARADO

This is an important opportunity to inform the OAS about the environmental policy we are designing in Chile. One of my government's aims in that policy is to seek agreement and consensus. I believe that the OAS today has the ability and potential to serve as a common forum for achieving certain agreements and consensus, which are necessary as much in this field of the environment as in others in the international sphere.

There are three basic tasks that Chile is addressing. These have been entrusted by President Aylwin to the National Environmental Commission, which I chair as minister of national assets.

The first task is to design an environmental policy; the second is to draft an environmental code; and the third is to put forward an institutional proposal that will make our policy efficient and our environmental law effective.

Until now, Chile has had no environmental policy or code. Instead, we have a number of legal provisions scattered among the various parts of our legal system. Nor are there institutions that deal directly with the environment issue—so the overall picture is rather depressing and complicated, but it is also a challenge we are prepared to tackle.

The positive perspective shows us that starting from zero is perhaps an advantage: it enables us to develop an overall conception from the outset instead of struggling with an accumulation of disconnected and disorganized parts.

The purpose of my presentation is to explain what we are doing to design our national environmental policy.

We first agreed that our environmental policy must be based on clear principles. An environmental policy must have principles that delineate the framework of the policy. I will mention only some of the principles that seem to me to be the most important.

The first principle on which our environmental policy is based is very general and quasi-philosophical, but it is enormously significant for the subsequent prospects of that policy, namely respect for nature. We are immersed in a civilization where nature has been subordinated by man, where the relationship of man to nature, or, if you will, the relationship of society to land, is one of subordination. Nature is dominated; land is subordinated.

The relevant question here is whether it is possible to change or try to change that relationship. I realize, of course, that environmental policy in a country such as Chile cannot be scaled so pretentiously as to endeavor to make a real change in civilization. It is true that changing the relationship of man to nature and the relationship of society to land involves a change in civilization. However, on the eve of the twenty-first century, we must view this issue from that perspective and accept the challenge that humanity faces today to try to make that kind of change.

For Chile, this is especially important. Chile is undergoing profound democratic reconstruction. I believe it is possible to consider today whether a democratic relationship can also be established between man and nature. This involves an outlook of solidarity by our generation toward future generations. We cannot exhaust available natural resources for our own development and leave without any support base those who will have the task of going forward after us.

A second guiding principle of our environmental policy is environmental conservation. Here the challenge must be met by science and technology. Unlike the previous principle having to do with the ethics of cultural patterns, the principle of conservation is a challenge for scientific and technical development that we must place in the service of conservation. I am using conservation in the generally accepted sense of a rational equation between using and protecting resources.

In Chile, we are betting, in the design of our environmental policy, that it is possible to find a scientific-technical equation that will harmonize utilization and protection of resources. Based on this principle, we have designed the Chilean government's position on resources treatment and use and on environmental protection in the Antarctic continent.

It is true that if one adopts the minerals exploitation systems used in the other continents, catastrophic effects may well occur in Antarctica. But we are absolutely convinced, assuming there is scientific and technological progress, that it will be possible in the next 40 to 50 years for humanity to design productive structures, forms, and systems that will properly protect the environment. It is not necessarily true that there is only one way to produce or only one direction to go in establishing the conditions for exploiting resources. We believe rather that it is possible, using scientific and technological development, to design different ways to exploit our resources. This is a progressive vision of humanity.

Accordingly, I am especially interested in the proposal being studied by this commission to establish a center that will be able to collect information on everything being done in the scientific and technological fields in the Americas to achieve the conservation equation we require. There is a body of knowledge that must be arranged and coordinated, and I believe that at this point, because of the challenges we face in protecting the environment, concentrating all of our scientific and technological knowledge for environmental protection in an inter-American center is very important.

A third principle that we are considering in our environmental policy is energy conservation.

We start from the assumption that it is impossible for the developing world to achieve the present per capita energy consumption of the developed world. We would have to exhaust all of the planet's energy reserves if we tried to provide our people in a few years with the level of energy consumption that the developed countries have today.

Accordingly, the obvious conclusion is that we must rationalize the use of our energy sources, introduce ways to save energy, and finally seek alternate energy sources. It is also necessary to consider something that is inherent in this principle. What is involved in the final analysis when we consider energy savings is that we must begin to keep our development accounts from the perspective of other dimensions. Our national accounts are able to determine how much it costs to produce, or what the actual yields are in using various resources to arrive at an end product. However, we do not yet know the cost of destroying what must be used as an input for production, nor do we know how much it costs today to recover exhausted ecosystems or the ecosystems at high risk. And the only way to find out the cost is by keeping an energy balance sheet.

The issue is quite controversial, and obviously must be discussed, but it would appear that today we can operate all of our productive machinery while using 40 percent less energy than is now consumed.

Everything that points toward energy savings is not merely a matter of conserving energy but of reducing production costs and the pressure on the renewable or nonrenewable natural resources that provide the energy we use today.

This principle points not only to the entire production apparatus, but also to very different environments that are extremely complex.

If we want to save energy we must adopt a wide range of initiatives, from changing our domestic habits individually and collectively to introducing systematic and widespread recycling in the productive processes in many industrial subsectors.

The principle of energy conservation therefore has extremely diverse ramifications, which in due course must also be managed institutionally and also legally.

A fourth principle underlying our environmental policy is the promotion of all activities involving improvement in the quality of life. I will not dwell on a subject that today is taken for granted by all our governments: the close relationship between poverty and environmental degradation. Unless we solve the problems of large pockets of poverty, we will not be able to overcome the environmental problems that are increasing because of them.

We know perfectly well that poverty places pressure on the indiscriminate and irrational use of resources, and that there is no other alternative for the poor but to use resources in that way. They have no other way to survive, and it is impossible today even to consider other ways. However, if we are aware of the close relationship between poverty and environmental degradation, our environmental policy must encourage all efforts and programs to combat poverty.

Finally, another principle is that it is our responsibility to contribute as a country to overcoming worldwide environmental problems.

There is no need to look for the guilty ones. Looking for the guilty and pointing to the dimensions of their guilt is not what should guide our conduct. We should instead be able to establish a system of responsibilities where, in one way or another, contributions are rationally shared.

The only limit on the dimension of our responsibility is recognition by the industrialized countries of the North of their own responsibility in this area. If we adopt that perspective, the burdens can be shared responsibly by both. It is true that the contributions cannot be equal. But it is also true that the responsibilities are shared. And if we do not take that approach, I believe we are not going to be able to resolve the worldwide problems that objectively end up affecting all of us, even those who believe that the guilty must be sought out.

From that perspective, therefore, we are concerned that on the eve of the World Conference on the Environment and Development to be held in Brazil, there is an atmosphere of tension and growing conflicts of interests between the countries of the North and the South. If we do not make an effort to overcome that tension, we will divide ourselves into the guilty and the victims and gain nothing, because we are all going to be affected equally by these problems.

Having discussed some of the principles of our environmental policy, I would like to mention a group of minimum instruments required to implement that policy.

The first instrument we need is an environmental authority; that is, there is a need to decide where the state apparatus should be located and what kind of attributes it should have. There is controversy about this in Chile, and I know that is true in other countries of the Americas also. One side says that, in view of the conceptual and theoretical nature of environmental problems— their presence everywhere and their extraordinary extension—only mechanisms for intersectoral or interinstitutional coordination can be considered.

If we compare this assertion with the need to give environmental officials executive power, we find that it contradicts the principle of intersectoral coordination. There are no coordinating apparatuses that are actually capable of exercising authority. Their limit is precisely their definition. They are coordinating and not decisionmaking apparatuses. So in this dilemma, faced with the urgency and seriousness of environmental problems, it is better to give priority to having an authority with executive power, and, essentially, that means having ministries. The ministries are where the highest executive powers lie. I believe that if we require an instrument with authority, that instrument must be a ministry.

The second instrument our countries must have is environmental monitoring and information systems. There is no way to carry out effective environmental activities if they are not based on precise diagnoses. And to make those diagnoses, we must have environmental monitoring and information systems, which we do not have today. We must make specific efforts to gather data, which, in our countries, are scattered in statistical institutes, natural resource centers, or ministries. But the conceptual design of information suitable for environmental decisionmaking is different. It is a special design, using known technology, so we do not have to look very far to find it. Monitoring and information systems should ideally be shared among all countries. Information anarchy among the various countries could make any hemisphere-wide action program ineffective.

Accordingly, this instrument of environmental monitoring and information systems based on a common conceptual design becomes an elementary requirement at this time. A specific program aimed at the convergence of our information systems is needed. I believe we are in a position to standardize and unify our information systems to make effective hemisphere-wide policies.

The last instrument is extremely important. It involves measurement of the adverse effects all activities have on the environment. We lack environmental quality standards differentiated for the various subsectors of productive activities—standards that must be compatible with the development level of the productive and technological forces of our countries.

We have to make an especially great effort in Chile to design these standards conceptually and then create practical apparatuses capable of taking measures in each of the productive activities to see whether we are meeting those standards. Usually, we import conceptual designs or standards designed conceptually in other countries. Chile has been using the Environmental Protection Agency standards, and if they were to be applied rigorously, 70 to 80 percent of productive activities in Chile would have to be shut down.

Therefore, we need to establish standards appropriate to the development level of the productive and technological forces of our countries. But we also need an agreed-upon system of regulations that prevents unfair competition by price reductions or standards increases among the countries.

Today our countries are competing in international markets by selling primary products requiring compliance with certain environmental quality standards, both in their productive systems and in the end product. We therefore need a system of conventions that do not take advantage of any gap there may be in environmental quality standards between countries. It is also worthwhile to make a collective effort through some of the specific programs that can be given impetus by the Organization of American States, because this is not primarily a technical problem; it is actually a political problem.

We have adopted in Chile the working method of seeking agreements and consensus among the various sectors. What we are doing today is coordinating the interests of private and public enterprises, government agencies, scientific societies, academies concerned with the environment, and, most importantly, citizens' organizations concerned with environmental issues. We are constantly seeking agreement and consensus among these four types of institutions: businesses, government, scientific and academic institutions, and citizen and social organizations.

The method is slow and gradual, but it produces an enormous yield, for all decisions are made with a maximum of legitimacy. Ensuring legitimacy for environmental problems requires that government decisions not be conceived exclusively by the executive branch or the authorities, but that they emerge from a national consensus.

Chile is a country that has experienced strong economic growth in recent years. However, from the perspective I must have as a minister dealing with environmental issues, I believe that growth must be achieved with proper protection and management of our natural resources. The only guarantee of future sustainable development is to make growth, social justice, and environmental protection compatible with one another. The democratic government of Chile is aiming in that direction, and I hope we will be successful.

Note: This chapter was delivered in a slightly different form as an address by Luis Alvarado, Chilean minister of national assets, to the special working group on the environment of the OAS at its meeting of November 26, 1990.

A Commitment to Life

MOSTAFA K. TOLBA

Colombian-born author Gabriel García Marquéz, in describing the spreading wastelands of deforestation, wrote of how "fifty years of uncontrolled deforestation had destroyed [the Great Magdalena River Valley]: the boilers of the riverboats had consumed the thick forest; . . . the hunters of skins had exterminated the alligators; the parrots and monkeys had died out as the foliage was destroyed."

There can be no doubt our life-supporting biosphere will not withstand another fifty years—or even much less—of ecological devastation. Time is running out. In response, people and governments everywhere—and this region is certainly no exception—are calling for action to build environmentally sound and sustainable development.

As the recent IADP/UNDP report, *Our Own Agenda*, clearly argues, "On Earth, there can be no Third World." We share one single planet. Our planetary survival demands that governments pull together to confront not merely the symptoms of ecological destruction—from the threat of climate change and the proliferation of hazardous wastes to the destruction of tropical and temperate forests—but more importantly, their underlying economic and societal *causes*.

Indeed, the Brasilia Declaration cogently highlights the inseparable link between this region's economic and development crisis and its grave environmental problems. Poverty, unfair international economic conditions, and crippling debt are structural problems creating and strengthening the stranglehold of natural resource destruction and growing pollution.

Determination to forge collective solutions to shared economic and environmental problems has moved closer to reality. Progress in crafting an effective, concrete regional action plan has been remarkable. Governments and multilateral and regional organizations—together with the core working group of ECLAC, Inter-American Development Bank, UNEP, and UNDP—have engaged in intensive consultations. We all have been united in our determination to ensure it is a plan developed by Latin American and Caribbean governments for the benefit of Latin American and Caribbean people. The action plan is based on the premise of international cooperation and a concrete commitment to global partnership. It endeavors to strike a balance between collective strategies and the sovereign right of each nation to freely manage its natural resources.

Such a plan is born of necessity. It is born of the urgent need to tackle escalating ecological problems—themselves born of unprecedented regional changes in agriculture, industry, transportation, energy consumption, and urbanization—all in a very short time. Many changes have been welcome. Impressive gains have been made in public health, education, and life expectancy, to name just a few. Too often, however, flawed development patterns have only deepened the development and environmental crisis. For example, an estimated 163 million people currently live in poverty in the region, of which 61 million are sentenced to extreme poverty. Real per capita Gross Domestic Product in many countries has fallen during what has been called the "lost decade" of development. Today, the problems of uneven economic distribution, hyper-inflation, lawlessness, swelling shantytowns, and tragic armies of homeless infants are just some of the prices of past mistakes.

Only recently have we clearly understood that flawed development is often the cause, not the cure, of resource mismanagement and ecological destruction. There is no need for a full rehearsal of all the environmental problems facing this region. You know them much better than I do. But you may agree ecological problems are overshadowed by deforestation and the ensuing loss of biological patrimony, the impact of environmental deterioration on human settlements, inappropriate land use, and the over-exploitation and pollution of marine resources.

I will first focus on tropical deforestation. *The Brazilian Secretariat of Science and Technology* estimates that from 1976 to 1989, the average rate of deforestation in the Amazonian region was 21,800 square kilometers per year. In 1989, the total deforested area was 394,000 square kilometers, and 93,000 of those were deforested before 1974.

Recent reports suggest global tropical deforestation may be twice as bad as previously estimated. Estimates indicate that as much as 1.5 acres of tropical forests are lost each second around the world. In this region, some estimates indicate that an area larger than Mexico has disappeared through burning and clearing in the last three decades. Estimates, however, vary widely. Thus a first priority action in this area is to intensify scientific monitoring and assessment of deforestation rates.

Resource destruction has—as you are fully aware—profound repercussions on future regional economic growth. One such repercussion is the accelerating extinction of the region's biodiversity. Untapped, undiscovered plant and animal resources face extinction. The industrialized world will have to come back to this and other tropical regions of the world for plant breeding, new medicines, and the inevitable boom in biotechnology. Efforts must be redoubled to conserve these precious resources.

Effort is likewise needed to address the rapid rise in urbanization. Three of four people in the region currently live in urban areas. As always, it is the poor and the underprivileged who suffer most. Living in overcrowded shantytowns and slums, they suffer from unsanitary home and working conditions. They lack clean water and sewer systems. Hundreds of thousands of urban immigrants are drawn each year to overcrowded cities, unable to cope with spiralling hazardous wastes, acid rain, and airborne pollution. In Mexico City, deaths attributed to cancer, influenza, and pneumonia have risen six-fold since 1956. On a regional basis, an estimated 81 million people face serious urban air pollution, leading to 2.3 million cases of chronic respiratory illness among children and over 100,000 cases of chronic bronchitis among the elderly. Yet no statistic can convey the despair and suffering of people living in slums.

Such problems will only increase as "mega cities" of 30 million people or more spring up throughout the region in the next century. Political will is needed to create frameworks for sound urban planning and to improve the provision of land to the poor by, for example, granting security of tenure on illegally settled plots or providing cheap loans and serviced housing plots.

Another priority area concerns the use of land resources to enlarge agricultural frontiers. Modest gains in agricultural productivity over the recent years were largely fueled through excessive use of fertilizers and pesticides. The once exponential rise in crop yields is approaching a plateau because of limits of the "Green Revolution" and excessive use of agrochemicals that are prompting soil pollution and exhaustion. Experience shows that by reforming land practices, involving rural communities, and advancing agroforestry, mixed and traditional cropping, integrated pest management, and other approaches, agricultural yields can increase in a sustainable way.

Brazil's President Fernando Collor de Mello recently summed up this region's determination to environmental protection, by stating "On questions of ecology, we have made a fundamental commitment to life. We have nothing to hide and nothing to explain" (*Time*, July 1990).

This is the sort of commitment that leads us all into bringing forward meaningful, lasting solutions. And to do that we must address the economic and social forces creating environmental destruction and thereby jeopardizing the prospects of development and economic growth. I have already mentioned poverty, unfair international economic relations, and debt. There are other forces: uneven population growth, unsound agricultural practices, unplanned expansion of agricultural frontiers, the insatiable international demand for limited and precious natural resources such as high-grade tropical timbers, and inappropriate land tenure policies.

I am aware plans have been in place at the national and regional levels to combat deforestation and put the development of tropical forests on solid, sustainable grounds. More countries in the Latin American and Caribbean region have national forestry action plans than any other region of the world.

To address the socio-economic forces, progress is needed in economic reforms on at least two fronts:

The *first* front is on a national level. Despite serious efforts by national environmental departments, current fiscal and monetary policies—ranging from incentives to tax shelters—continue to encourage cattle ranchers, small-scale farmers, settlers, city developers, industrialists, and energy authorities to expand commercial operations at the expense of the environment and the national resource base.

Such economic policies are certainly not the monopoly of this region. Virtually all countries need to align fiscal, transportation, energy, trade, development, and other policies with environmental goals. Success probably depends on articulating environmental arguments to economic decisionmakers in their own language. This is an area where ECLAC, in cooperation with UNEP, has been pursuing a series of detailed studies, the results of which I hope will fully be used during the implementation of the agreed-upon regional action plan.

An extremely important factor in this economic equation is finding a realistic symmetry between the prices of goods and services and their real ecological and social costs. To date, governments do not provide industry and people with incentives *not* to destroy the environment, largely because conservation is still not viewed as a legitimate form of economic development. Immediate benefits are gained from turning jungles into pasture or razing a mangrove swamp for building materials. The full social and economic costs of such actions are transferred to society as a whole, concealed in national accounts and passed on to the next generation.

We have to expose the full social and ecological costs of destruction. Market forces simply have not provided sufficient incentives to promote environmental protection. Assessments of national wealth accommodate trees when they are cut, harvests when gathered, and fish when sold. But they cannot assess the value of intact forests, the soils on which crops are grown, and the mangroves, coral reefs, and other marine ecosystems that support marine life.

In short, most market economies perpetuate a system of *perverse* incentives, with scarce means to measure the direct value of healthy ecosystems, and even less to assess the indirect value of ecosystem functions such as watershed protection, photosynthesis, climate regulation, and soil fertility, and with even lesser means to assess the value of these natural resources to future generations.

That must change. To do so, some cherished ideas about the marketplace must go by the board. Government intervention is required in order to provide economic incentives—equitably applied—to halt the over-exploitation of precious renewable natural resources.

Governments should reassess budget priorities to ensure that subsidies, infrastructure projects, energy pricing policies, and fiscal and trade policies actively promote environmental protection. And innovative revenue-generating mechanisms including green taxes, charges on so-called "free" natural resources like clean air and water, user fees, pricing adjustments, concessionary loans, and rebates need to be introduced. Such tools, while generating new public funds for environmental protection, also encourage behavioral changes by rewarding action toward environmental protection and by penalizing polluting enterprises.

The *second* economic front is on an international level. Of all economic problems facing the region, none is more ominous than the debt crisis. It continues to drain national treasuries, consume foreign exchange export earnings, and dash individual hopes for future growth and a better life. Interest payments of $200 billion between 1982 and 1989 were too often financed by rapid exploitation of natural resources to meet crushing debt-servicing obligations. Even with such over-exploitation, scarce little remains to meet the growing costs of proper resource management and sustainable development.

This can neither be maintained nor continued. The case must be made for sustantially increased debt write-off. There is nothing new in this; it has been a goal for some time.

We also need to build the case—as the Brasilia Declaration suggests—for concrete, objective, and automatic financial commitments, and for the provision of *new and additional* financial and other resources to promote environmental protection. This region has the political commitment, public support, skills, and traditions to save its environment. Additional financial resources and the transfer of proper technology is needed to be able to carry the task at hand.

Despite enormous obstacles, progress toward global partnership is being made. At UNEP's 1990 special session of the governing council, at the preparatory committee meeting for the UN conference on environment and development, and at numerous conferences and international meetings, the world community has voiced strong support for cooperative action. Too many economic roadblocks already exist without the environmental agenda becoming another.

There is evidence that governments will back up words with deeds. Four months ago in London, nearly 100 countries from north, south, east, and west created a Multilateral Ozone Fund of $160 million over three years—to grow to $240 million when other developing countries become parties to the Montreal Protocol. This fund—the first ever created to address a specific global environmental problem—will assist developing countries in becoming full partners in protecting the ozone layer by acquiring CFC substitute chemicals and technologies without confronting more economic roadblocks.

Another step toward action is the World Bank's work with UNDP and UNEP to shape the modalities for a global environmental facility which would provide $1 billion in special drawing rights for a three-year period to finance developing countries' environmental efforts to save the ozone layer, address climate change, improve water development, and protect biodiversity.

Cooperation in the environmental field is not novel to this region. In fact, this is the first region to have organized—in the developing world— regional ministerial conferences to agree upon common actions to deal with common problems.

The Convention and Action Plan for the Protection and Development of the Marine Environment of the Wider Caribbean Region is a pioneer among the regional seas activities in the world. That plan, and the Plan of Action for the South-East Pacific, have been highly successful regional strategies to address shared environmental problems. Both have worked to find the balance between urgently needed economic development and the protection and preservation of the marine environment.

And as *Our Own Agenda* argues, the Latin American and Caribbean region is contributing to the global debate on sustainable development. Solutions geared to the region are being forged—solutions that develop both environmental and economic resources and enshrine the principle of equitable growth.

Determination to define a course of development-sustainability that meets the needs and taps the wisdom of this region likewise underlines the approach which helped shape the proposed regional action plan. It is designed to integrate environmental considerations at the outset of development activities, whereby planners and economic policymakers regard ecological protection as an indispensable component of economic, social, and cultural development.

At the national level, the plan is geared to reinforce environmental administrations and institutions, including the development of environmental legislation and the broad-based participation of community groups, the private sector, and individuals.

At the regional level, the plan seeks cooperation in responding to regional and subregional problems of common concern by way of coordinating and enhancing regional scientific research, monitoring and assessment capabilities, and the exchange of data on natural resource endowment and management strategies, in order to avoid overlaps and unnecessary duplication of efforts.

The proposed plan is intended to complement—not replace—ongoing regional efforts. It is to strengthen such critical regional programs as development and environmental planning; environmental legislation and institutional frameworks; environmental education; the protection and conservation of the natural and cultural heritage and of protected areas; the environmental training network; and the action plan for the south-east Pacific and the Wider Caribbean Environment Program.

The plan also calls for new initiatives, including the creation and coordination of a regional environmental information service and specific means to promote technology transfer.

Sustainable fresh water management should also be a key goal of the action plan. This region is the largest repository of fresh water in the developing world, and the largest repository of international fresh water resources anywhere in the world. I proposed to the preparatory committee of UNCED at its Nairobi meeting that governments should consider supporting the design and implementation of a pilot project for the cooperative management of an international water course in Latin America. I suggest that this, together with other specific pilot projects for other regions of the world, be presented to UNCED, each identifying specific targets over specific periods of time, costing the required activities, and indicating from where the financial resources could come.

That proposal could be taken up within the action plan, together with regional strategies, to address global environmental problems of climate change, ozone layer depletion, conservation of biodiversity, and minimization of hazardous wastes. The problems of climate change and biodiversity are soon to be addressed in global treaties being drafted. Both will have important implications for this region. Popular views on them are of great importance in charting the path toward achieving meaningful treaties. The target date is Rio de Janciro in 1992. But certainly that target should not be met at the expanse of the substance and clear definition of the responsibilities of individual countries and groups of countries to global action.

To ensure the regional plan moves from ideas to results, experts have elaborated clear decisionmaking and administrative mechanisms, beginning with the regional ministerial meetings, to the regional intergovernmental committee, and five support and advisory committees—each with clearly delineated duties. To coordinate the implementation of the action plan, UNEP's regional office for Latin America and the Caribbean—if called upon—can act as the secretariat for that purpose. UNEP's support of the implementation of the action plan could be reflected in the 1992–1993 proposed program budget for consideration by the governing council in 1991. And if called upon to do so, UNEP can ensure that all UNEP-supported projects for the Latin American and Caribbean region will be required in the future to fall under the auspices of the action plan and according to the priorities set for its implementation.

This region is blessed beyond imagination with remarkable secrets of the natural order. It is our moral and ethical duty to protect God's creation, to ensure we leave to our children a nourishing planet earth. That is the commitment to life and ecological protection I know we all share.

Note: This chapter was delivered in a slightly different form as an address by Mostafa K. Tolba, executive director of the United Nations Environment Programme, to the seventh ministerial meeting of the Latin American and Caribbean region, Port-of-Spain, October 22, 1990.

Inter-American Program of Action for Environmental Protection

AG/RES. 1114 (XXI-0/91. Resolution adopted at the eleventh plenary session, held on June 8, 1991.)

THE GENERAL ASSEMBLY,

HAVING SEEN the report of the Permanent Council on the establishment of an inter-American system for nature conservation (AG/doc.2718/91);

CONSIDERING that the diverse dimensions of the ecological crisis call for renewed and more effective solidarity between the states at the subregional, regional, and world levels;

RECALLING:

That the Charter of the Organization of American States establishes in its preamble that the "historic mission of America is to offer to man a land of liberty and a favorable environment for the development of his personality and the realization of his just aspirations";

That, in Article 30, it provides that "inter-American cooperation for integral development is the common and joint responsibility of the Member States . . .";

That, in Article 29, it establishes that "the Member States, inspired by the principles of inter-American solidarity and cooperation, pledge themselves to a united effort to ensure international social justice in their relations and integral development for their peoples . . . "; and

That, in Article 37, it provides that "the Member States shall extend among themselves the benefits of science and technology . . . "; and

BEARING IN MIND the views expressed in the Declaration of Brasilia (Sixth Ministerial Meeting on the Environment in Latin America and the Caribbean, 1989); the Amazon Declaration (First Meeting of the Presidents of the Countries of the Amazon Region, 1989); the Declaration of San Francisco de Quito (Third Meeting of Ministers of Foreign Affairs of the States Parties to the Treaty for Amazonian Cooperation, 1989); the Call to Action (Seventh Meeting of Ministers on the Environment for Latin America and the Caribbean, Trinidad and Tobago, 1990); the

Declaration of Puntarenas (Meeting of the Central American Presidents in Puntarenas, Costa Rica, 1991); the Tlatelolco Platform on Environment and Development (Regional Meeting for Latin America and the Caribbean, Preparatory to the United Nations Conference on Environment and Development—ENCED—Mexico, 1991); and other instruments signed by the OAS member states with international organizations outside the region on environmental matters,

RESOLVES:

1. To note with satisfaction the report presented by the Permanent Council on the establishment of an inter-American system for environmental protection.

2. To adopt the following Program of Action:

INTER-AMERICAN PROGRAM OF ACTION FOR ENVIRONMENTAL PROTECTION

The member states of the Organization of American States, with a view to protecting and improving the environment, resolve to adopt as guidelines for pursuing the objectives of this Program of Action the principles of Article 3 of the Charter of the Organization of American States, those enshrined in the Declaration issued at the United Nations Conference on the Human Environment (Stockholm, 1972), and those adopted by the United Nations General Assembly in preparation for the Conference on Environment and Development (Rio de Janeiro, 1992).

In accordance with those principles, the following objectives are adopted for the Inter-American Program of Action for Environmental Protection:

I. Objectives

a. To use the OAS as a forum for a rational, constructive hemisphere-wide debate, free of recrimination, aimed at developing a specific regional approach in order to contribute to implementation of the proposals of global scope that environmental protection requires.

b. To help derive maximum advantage from international sectoral efforts by identifying and addressing individually or collectively, as appropriate, the problems of conservation and protection of the environment in the Americas, for purposes that include dealing with abject poverty and its connection with environmental degradation.

c. To promote OAS participation in agreeing upon a regional position on other meetings and initiatives, whether regional or worldwide, on environmental protection.

d. To support the framing of ecologically balanced and culturally viable environmental policies that reconcile development, conservation, and the rational, sustained use of the environment and natural resources, including a policy on the transfer of nonpolluting technologies.

e. To promote cooperation among the member states for the provision of mutual technical and institutional assistance in the framing of policies, planning, implementing activities, surveillance, and exchanges of information, in order to maintain, restore, and improve the quality of the environment.

f. To promote cooperation and communication among the OAS member states on environmental problems, including technology transfer, the development of standardized terminology, the establishment of common criteria, and the implementation of joint projects for the defense of protected areas and for resource management and control.

g. To sponsor and support projects for the design and use of technologies that further environmental protection.

h. To promote the development and progressive codification of environmental law and to seek, insofar as possible, to harmonize such legislation among the countries of the hemisphere, to bring about sustainable development, bearing in mind the specific needs and characteristics of each country.

i. To promote cooperation among the member states to develop further the body of international law regarding liability and compensation for the victims of pollution and other environmental damage caused by activities within the jurisdiction or control of such states to areas beyond their jurisdictions.

j. To cooperate in the study and identification of the possible effects on the environment of the illicit use and production of narcotic drugs and psychotropic substances and traffic therein.

k. To promote in the inter-American sphere better knowledge and understanding of the region's environmental problems and of the advantages of an integrated conservation strategy.

l. To encourage the media to support regional and national efforts to create environmental awareness and better educate and inform people on the need to protect the environment in order to allow the full development of present and future generations in the Americas.

m. To promote the coordinated participation of nongovernmental organizations and those from other sectors of society in designing and implementing measures to protect and improve the environment and bring about sustainable development.

II. Measures Directed at the Member States

It is recommended that the member states adopt the following measures in order to achieve the objectives of this Program:

a. The adaptation, in exercise of the sovereignty of the states over its natural resources, of government institutions to enable them to coordinate, unify, and strengthen environmental management; in particular, consideration of the possibility of creating environmental ministries, agencies, or high-level national mechanisms on the environment to exercise general coordination, oversight, control, and monitoring of efforts to preserve and use in a sustainable way its environmental heritage.

b. Promotion of the responsible use of natural resources in the development of productive activities that favor economic growth. In particular, promotion of efficient energy use and the use of renewable energy sources.

c. Study of the possibility of revising national accounts in light of the experience of countries that keep national environmental accounts, so as to incorporate into them the impact produced by natural resource use.

d. In adopting standards on the environment and the preservation of ecosystems, avoidance, in accordance with the provisions of the GATT, of the imposition of nontariff barriers that could distort trade; also, measures to ensure that the addition of environmental standards and strategies in national planning does not place new types of conditions on development assistance or financing.

e. In accordance with applicable law, requiring environmental impact studies in the planning of investment projects by private or public enterprises, whether domestic or foreign, to be completed before they materialize, so as to determine any significant adverse effect on the environment, on the health and welfare of the population, or on the national wealth of the country in question.

f. The study and preparation of integrated programs for the preservation and management of biodiversity, without prejudice to the sovereignty of states over their natural resources, the exploration of new mechanisms, such as monetary contributions from enterprises toward the conservation of the species which they use and which, until now, have been evaluated in a conventional way that disregards their value as an asset of the country that possesses that resource.

g. Promotion of policies that include, among other aspects, economic incentives for environmental protection.

h. Promotion of measures aimed at avoiding transborder pollution and at restricting and controlling the transboundary carriage of hazardous wastes and impeding their illegal transport.

i. Prevention of the indiscriminate discharge of toxic and hazardous wastes into lakes, rivers, coastal waters, and oceans with the ensuing hazards to those areas, and increased efforts to check the phenomenon of acid rain.

j. Adoption, revision, or consolidation of national environmental laws, so that conservation and sustainable development are complementary, and the establishment of national mechanisms for prevention and for monitoring compliance with environmental laws.

k. The adoption of bilateral or multilateral agreements, as appropriate, for cross-border cooperation in environmental matters.

l. Encouragement of international cooperation and concerted action toward developing joint biotechnology programs that will contribute to preserving biological diversity and to generating high-value-added projects.

m. Recognition that it is their shared responsibility to protect the environment, and that the developed countries should support, in addition to existing programs, increased flows of capital and of nonpolluting technologies to the developing countries through international cooperation, in order to ensure their full participation in the international efforts to protect the environment and promote sustainable development.

III. Measures for Regional Cooperation

In order to assist the member states in regional cooperation to implement actions and adopt measures for the protection and improvement of the environment, it is recommended that the Permanent Council establish a Standing Committee through which the OAS might serve as an effective forum for proposing the Organization's environmental policy, and develop, coordinate, evaluate, and monitor the following measures, among others:

a. Compilation of indexes of information available on the natural resource base of the Americas, as well as of economic and physical indicators of the state of the environment.

b. Promotion of increased cooperation between the developed and developing countries of the hemisphere, and especially, the transfer to the latter of modern, environmentally sound technologies on terms that foster their wide dissemination without constituting an excessive economic burden on the developing countries; of particular importance are technologies that facilitate energy savings, especially in the transportation sector, as well as financing for those purposes, in order to replace technologies whose environmental consequences are more costly than their replacement.

c. Promotion of cooperation by the countries of the hemisphere in global efforts to deal with the effects of climatic changes and, under the Montreal Protocol, to reduce substances that deplete the ozone layer, and in particular, the examination of possible joint hemispheric action to broaden and strengthen that cooperation, with particular regard to the situation of the developing countries most severely affected by the depletion of the ozone layer.

d. Promotion of intergovernmental cooperation to support the sustainable management of the forestry ecosystems, including appropriate financial assistance and the transfer of technologies, as well as the formulation of integrated programs for the protection, rational use, and restoration of those ecosystems.

e. Encouragement for the design of regional policies on accident prevention and on the carriage and disposal of radioactive, toxic, and hazardous wastes or materials, in accordance with the applicable international legal instruments.

f. Collaboration with requesting member states in the development of their scientific research capabilities, preferably *in situ*, to enable them to manage their ecosystems more efficiently and strengthen processes for arriving at environmentally sound decisions.

g. Promotion of a greater environmental awareness as a dimension and omnipresent function of education, from an interdisciplinary standpoint, in the member states of the inter-American system.

h. Promotion of and support for manpower training in order to develop professional and technical personnel in scientific, technical, legal, administrative, economic, and educational aspects of conservation in the hemisphere.

i. Support for and promotion of the inclusion of environmental considerations in development planning and in the formulation of investment projects.

j. Provision of technical support and advisory services to requesting member states to assist in the conclusion of agreements and projects for environmental protection and improvement, drawing on funds that may become available from likely reductions of the external debt, for example, those envisaged in the Enterprise for the Americas Initiative.

k. Promotion of cooperation among member states in the management and use of natural resources in shared ecosystems, and the provision, at the request of interested member states, of advisory services and technical support for these purposes.

l. The provision of advisory services and technical support to requesting member states in the prevention, reduction, or avoidance of adverse effects from transboundary pollution, including the transboundary movement or discharge of hazardous wastes.

m. Promotion of the coordination of policies for the conservation of fishery resources in order to protect, in particular, ecosystems that are fragile and vulnerable.

n. Study of the economic consequences of the degradation of coastal environments and the formulation of hemispheric cooperation strategies for the protection and restoration of marine, insular, and coastal ecosystems.

o. Collaboration with global, regional, and subregional efforts and programs concerning the seas, to conserve marine resources and protect the marine environment, including efforts and programs aimed at avoiding environmental pollution and the effects caused by hazardous and toxic wastes and radioactive substances coming from all sources, including those of nuclear origin.

p. Promotion of new hemisphere-wide projects for the creation and management of parks and reserves for the preservation of ecosystems, habitats, and natural monuments; consideration of new methods for evaluating the cultural, social and economic benefits of those areas with a view to making them more self-supporting.

q. Support for requesting member states in the formulation of projects to improve energy efficiency and the use of alternative energy resources, especially those that use renewable resources, and encouragement for international financial institutions to allocate more resources and establish special facilities for the expansion of investments for those purposes.

r. Request that the Inter-American Juridical Committee prepare reference indexes on the environmental legislation of the various countries, with the cooperation of the General Secretariat.

s. Promotion of the adoption within the region of agreements, conventions, and treaties for the conservation of ecosystems.

t. Promotion of the revision, in cooperation with the Inter-American Juridical Committee and the General Secretariat, of the 1940 Convention on Nature Protection and Wildlife Preservation in the Western Hemisphere by the introduction of new topics, such as the preservation of biodiversity; and study of the possibility of preparing an inter-American agreement for environmental conservation.

u. Promotion of the coordinated participation of nongovernmental organizations and other sectors of society in the regional effort to improve the environment and the quality of life in the region.

v. To promote, in coordination with CICAD, regional cooperation among the states in putting a stop to the possible adverse effects on the environment caused by the illicit use and production of narcotic drugs and psychotropic substances and traffic therein, by means of procedures such as illegal-crop substitution, that are not harmful to humans or the environment and would permit the rehabilitation of affected areas and the ecologically sustainable socioeconomic development of the region.

w. Performance, in coordination with CICAD, IICA, PAHO, and the IDB, of a study of the effects that the illicit use and production of narcotic drugs and psychotropic substances and traffic therein have on the environment, and study and recommendation of ecologically safe methods for the storage and destruction of the chemical substances used in their manufacture and for the replacement and eventual eradication of illegal crops, with a view to the rehabilitation and development of the local communities and affected ecosystems in the regions.

x. Maintenance of ongoing coordination with the relevant United Nations agencies and global, regional, and subregional efforts aimed at environmental conservation. Especially, cooperation in the preparatory work of the United Nations Conference on the Environment and Development to be held in Brazil in 1992 and adaptation of the work of the Committee to any prospective results of that Conference; also, preparation, in coordination with the Executive Secretaries of CIECC and CIES, of an analytical document on the status of the environment in the Americas, for presentation to that United Nations Conference on the Environment and Development.

y. Performance of a study with a view to establishing an inter-American center for environmental studies to collaborate in academic research and hemispheric thinking on conservation of the environment, and presentation of that study to the Permanent Council for consideration at the twenty-second regular session of the General Assembly. This Center would engage in the following activities:

    i.   The conduct of seminars, encounters, and studies for the presentation and exchange of experiences in connection with studies and strategies for the treatment of conservation as a vehicle for integrated development in the hemisphere.

    ii.   The regular dissemination of salient developments in problems of conservation in the Americas, and in projects and measures newly adopted by the states for protection of the environment.

    iii.   Establishment of an academic periodical for the publication of articles, developments in research, and discussions that illustrate the salient proposals and currents of thought in the field of ecosystem conservation.

    iv.   The conduct of research on environmental problems with an inter-American dimension.

    v.   The promotion in particular of interdisciplinary studies on, among other subjects, models for development, economics and environment, technology transfers, and environmental conservation, and on the legal, ethical, and social implications of conservation of the environment and biodiversity in the hemisphere.

    vi.   Assistance in generating and the study of environmental statistics on the countries of the hemisphere, taking account of the work done by other institutions on the subject, for the ultimate purpose of harmonizing them and thereby strengthening national and international policies on ecosystem conservation; collaboration in the performance of studies to facilitate the adoption of national environmental accounts in the countries of the region.

3. To establish an Inter-American Environment Day as part of a possible hemisphere-wide publicity campaign to foster environmental awareness, which would be entrusted to the Standing Committee of the Permanent Council and the General Secretariat, working in collaboration with the member states.

4. To allocate in the Organization's program-budget for the biennium 1992–1993, sufficient initial resources for the advancement of the Inter-American Program of Action for Environmental Protection.

5. To recommend to the Permanent Council that, in coordination with the General Secretariat, it seek financing from external sources for implementation of this program of action and, to that end, explore the possibility of creating an inter-American environmental fund or other alternative means of financing for environmental conservation and research in and the transfer of nonpolluting technologies, to be constituted with special contributions from the member states, the observer countries, other international agencies, and private sources.

6. To request that the bodies of the OAS, the Inter-American specialized organizations and the departments of the General Secretariat cooperate in the execution of this Program of Action.

7. To request that the Permanent Council, in collaboration with the General Secretariat, intensify cooperation and coordination between the operations of the Organization of American States in the area of environmental conservation and the initiatives of the appropriate United Nations agencies and subregional efforts for similar purposes, especially in relation to the plan of environmental action for Latin America and the Caribbean promoted by UNEP, the programs of the Permanent Committee of the South Pacific, and the preparatory work for the United Nations Conference on Environment and Development in 1992.

Appendix:
Selected Documents

The Declaration of Brasilia

The Ministers of State in charge of environmental management and the Representatives of the countries participating in the Sixth Ministerial Meeting on the Environment in Latin America and the Caribbean, held in Brasilia from March 30 through 31, 1989, have decided to conclude their deliberations with the following

DECLARATION OF BRASILIA

1. The countries of Latin America and the Caribbean recognize the imperative need to strike a balance between socioeconomic development and environmental protection and conservation through the proper management of natural resources and control of environmental impacts as a source of common concern to the countries of the region having the utmost priority. Such a recognition is a statement about the indissoluble relationship that exists between environmental affairs and socioeconomic development and about the obligation to ensure the rational exploitation of resources for the benefit of present and future generations.

2. The Ministers endorse the principle that each State has the sovereign right to administer freely its natural resources. This does not, however, exclude the need for international cooperation at the subregional, regional and world levels; rather, it reinforces it. The Ministers further emphasize that solving the external debt problem and establishing a new fair and equitable International Economic Order are essential conditions for securing democracy in Latin America and the Caribbean, promoting regional peace and security as well as sustained economic and social development, the only possible alternative for the rational use of our natural resources and meeting the needs of our peoples.

3. Improving economic and social conditions is the key to preventing the defacement of the environment in our countries. In Latin America and the Caribbean, as in other parts of the Third World, underdevelopment and the deterioration of the environment are factors in a vicious circle that condemns millions of people to a quality of life beneath the norms of human dignity.

4. The Ministers therefore resolve to step up efforts to further in their respective countries a greater understanding of the rightful relationships between economic development planning and environmental problems and concerns, and to consolidate and improve the effective national environmental management and planning capacity. However, the Ministers are of the opinion that current levels of economic development and growth rates severely curtail the likelihood of the proper environmental management and conservation objectives being met.

5. Further, this situation has been exacerbated by the severe

45

indebtedness of Latin America and the Caribbean vis-à-vis the financial community of the industrialized countries. The indebtedness crisis and the adjustment policies stemming from that crisis have eroded conditions for economic, social and environmental development. The debt cannot be paid under current conditions, not by increasing hunger and poverty among our peoples, not with further underdevelopment and the consequent defacement of our environment. Clearly, there must be a change in the current approach to the external debt and an immediate reversal brought about in the current process of the negative transfer of resources whereby the developing countries have become net exporters of capital to the developed countries.

6. The measures adopted by the countries of the region are important, but they are not enough to provide a fair, stable and lasting solution to the debt problem. Such a solution will only be possible if changes are made in the terms and conditions applying to treatment of the debt and if the creditors assume their share of the responsibility to solve together the problem of indebtedness and its consequences.

7. The international financial organizations must ensure, by means of specific financial facilities, that sufficient additional resources are made available, on concessionary terms, for the execution of environmental protection projects in the developing countries. In allocating resources for this purpose, conditions that will entail, in practice, a cut in available resources for environmental protection should not be imposed.

8. In light of the foregoing considerations, the Ministers are appealing to the industrialized countries, and particularly to those that share our concern about the effective management of the environment, to augment substantially the level of their technical and financial contributions to the developing countries and their effective support to the United Nations Environmental Programme.

9. In this regard, it is imperative that the countries of Latin America and the Caribbean enlist assistance, if and when they so request, in developing their scientific research capacity so that they may effectively manage their natural systems and strengthen national processes for making appropriate environmental decisions.

10. Furthermore, international cooperation for environmental protection should include free access to scientific information and to the nonprofit transfer of nonpollutant and environmental conservation technologies to the developing countries. Access to new environmental technologies cannot be subjugated to purely commercial interests. Besides, the international organizations should help the countries of the region to improve their monitoring systems and strengthen their capacity to meet international environmental protection standards they have adopted.

11. In this regard, an all-out effort must be made to increase natural area systems that are protected in the region, and to cease practices that are

highly inimical to the environment as, for example, transportation and the indiscriminate and illegal disposal of toxic substances and materials and the dumping of such substances in the oceans, which entail a risk to coastal areas, particularly those of the Caribbean islands.

12. The seriousness of the environmental problems facing the world today stems mainly from industrialization, consumer and disposal patterns in the developed countries, which are at the root of the rapid wear and tear on natural resources on the planet and the ever-increasing introduction of pollutants in the biosphere. The Ministers of Latin America and the Caribbean are committed to a course of action that will be able to prevent a repetition of the mistakes of those development patterns and of their consequences in our countries, and we urge the industrialized countries to assume full responsibility commensurate with their financial and technological resources to reverse the process of defacement of the environment.

13. Countries that have nuclear and other types of arms for massive destruction must cease immediately all tests and experiments with such arms and actively promote their elimination. Only thus will it be possible to safeguard the environment and protect it from the risk of ecological pollution and destruction. The resources that are economized thereby should be funnelled to promote social and economic development, according to the provisions emanating from the meetings of the United Nations System.

14. Therefore, in addition to mobilizing domestic efforts to map out and implement national environmental protection and conservation plans, the countries of Latin America and the Caribbean are bent upon strengthening cooperation in this area and requesting technical and financial cooperation from countries in other regions and the international organizations. The Ministers of the Latin American and Caribbean countries are convinced that a global solution to our threatened planet is to be found in a level of cooperation, hitherto unprecedented, between the industrialized and the developing countries in aid of coming generations.

The Amazon Declaration

The Presidents of the Member Countries of the Amazonian Co-operation Treaty, meeting in Manaus on May 6, 1989, for the purpose of undertaking a joint reflection on their common interests in the Amazon region and, in particular, on the future of co-operation for the development and protection of the rich heritage of their respective Amazon territories, adopted the following

AMAZON DECLARATION

1. In the spirit of friendship and understanding that inspires our fraternal dialogue, we affirm our willingness to give full political impetus to the concerted efforts being undertaken by our Governments within the framework of the Amazonian Co-operation Treaty, signed on July 3, 1978; and also within the framework of their bi-lateral relations, with a view to promoting co-operation between our countries in all areas of common interest for the sustainable development of the Amazon region. Therefore, we commit ourselves to give the necessary impetus to the decisions contained in the Declaration of San Francisco de Quito, adopted by our Ministers of External Relations on March 7, 1989.

2. Conscious of the importance of protecting the cultural, economic and ecological heritage of our Amazon regions and of the necessity of using this potential to promote the economic and social development of our peoples, we reiterate that our Amazon heritage must be preserved through the rational use of the resources of the region, so that present and future generations may benefit from this legacy of nature.

3. We express our support for the recently-created Special Commissions for the Environment and Indigenous Affairs, aimed at fostering development, conserving the natural resources, the environment and the respective Amazonian populations, and we reiterate our full respect for the right of indigenous populations of the Amazonian region to have adopted all measures aimed at maintaining and preserving the integrity of these human groups, their cultures and their ecological habitats, subject to the exercise of the right which is inherent in the sovereignty of each State. Furthermore, we reiterate our support for actions aimed at strengthening the institutional structure of the Amazonian Co-operation Treaty, in accordance with the Declaration of San Francisco de Quito.

4. We reaffirm the sovereign right of each country to freely manage its natural resources, bearing in mind the need for promoting the economic and social development of its people and the adequate conservation of the environment. In the exercise of our sovereign responsibility to define the best ways of using and conserving this wealth and in addition to our national efforts and to the co-operation among our countries, we express our

willingness to accept co-operation from countries in other regions of the world, as well as from international organizations which might contribute to the implementation of national and regional projects and programmes which we decide to freely adopt without external impositions, in accordance with the priorities of our Governments.

5. We recognize that the defense of our environment requires the study of measures, both bi-lateral and regional, to prevent contamination-causing accidents and deal with their consequences once they have occurred.

6. We stress that the protection and conservation of the environment in the Region, one of the essential objectives of the Amazonian Co-operation Treaty to which each of our nations is firmly committed, cannot be achieved without improvement of the distressing social and economic conditions that oppress our peoples and that are aggravated by an increasingly adverse international context.

7. We denounce the grave conditions of the foreign debt and of its service which transform us into net exporters of capital to the creditor countries, at the cost of intolerable sacrifices for our peoples. We reiterate that the debt cannot be paid on the present conditions and in the present circumstances and that the problem of debt should be dealt with on the principle of co-responsibility, in terms that permit the reactivation of the process of economic growth and development in each of our countries, an essential condition for the protection, conservation, exploitation and rational utilization of our natural heritage.

8. We emphasize the need that the concerns expressed in the highly-developed countries in relation to the conservation of the Amazon environment be translated into measures of co-operation in the financial and technological fields. We call for the establishment of new resource flows in additional and concessional terms to projects oriented to environmental protection in our countries, including pure and applied scientific research, and object to attempts to impose conditionalities in the allocation of international resources for development. We expect the establishment of conditions to allow free access to scientific knowledge, clean technologies and technologies to be used in environmental protection and reject any attempts made to use legitimate ecological concerns to realize commercial profits. This approach is based above all on the fact that the principal causes for the deterioration of the environment on a world-wide scale are the patterns of industrialization and consumption as well as waste in the developed countries.

9. Conscious of the global risks for human life and environmental quality represented by the existence of nuclear weapons and other weapons of mass destruction, and concerned with preserving our region from these dangers, we reaffirm the commitments our countries have made to use nuclear energy exclusively for peaceful purposes and we urge the countries that

possess nuclear weapons to immediately cease the testing of such weapons and to promote the progressive elimination of their arsenals. Likewise, we repudiate the deposit of radioactive and other toxic wastes which may harm the ecosystems in the Amazonian region. We stress the need for appropriate measures to be taken to reduce the risks of environmental contamination in the peaceful use of nuclear energy. Furthermore, we express our support for the aims and objectives of the Treaty for the Prohibition of Nuclear Weapons in Latin America.

10. Convinced of the need to intensify the process of consultation and dialogue among our countries on all issues regarding the development of the Region, including those set forth in the Amazonian Co-operation Treaty, and certain that our co-operation strengthens integration and solidarity in Latin America, we affirm our decision to unite efforts in a vigorous and pioneering joint action, aimed at ensuring a future of peace, co-operation and prosperity for the nations of the Amazon region. Therefore, we are deciding to meet yearly.

for the government of Brazil *José Sarney*	for the government of Colombia *Virgilio Barco*
for the government of Ecuador *Rodrigo Borja*	for the government of Guyana *Hugh Desmond Hoyte*
for the government of Peru *Alan García Pérez*	for the government of Suriname *Ramsewak Shankar*
for the government of Venezuela *Carlos Andrés Pérez*	for the government of Bolivia *Valentin Abecia Baldivieso*

Action Plan for the Environment in Latin America and the Caribbean

Approved by the Seventh Ministerial Meeting on the Environment in Latin America and the Caribbean, Port-of-Spain, Trinidad and Tobago (22–23 October 1990)

I. BACKGROUND

1. This Plan of Action for the Environment in Latin America and the Caribbean was requested from the United Nations Environment Programme (UNEP) by the Sixth Ministerial Meeting on the Environment in Latin America and the Caribbean (Brasilia, Brazil, 30–31 March, 1989)[1].

2. The Governments requested that this Plan be created in response to the numerous national, regional and global problems which are affecting environmental quality in the region and which can be better addressed through international co-operation. The evolving regional co-operation mechanism constituted by the intergovernmental forum and UNEP, known as the "Regional Co-operation System on Environmental Matters in Latin America and the Caribbean", showed pronounced insufficiency for fully addressing those problems. The conclusion was clear: the system would have to be strengthened, and one of the ways of achieving this would be through the implementation of a comprehensive Action Plan.

3. The Governments requested this Action Plan, since they recognized it was necessary to strengthen horizontal technical co-operation, to ensure continuity between intergovernmental meetings; to foster the adoption of regional agreements; to achieve greater participation on the part of the region in working on global environmental problems having regional repercussions; to increase the participation of the region's Governments in the process of planning the programme and budget of UNEP; and to improve the co-ordination and linkage of different environmental activities undertaken in the region by different international and regional bodies.

4. In addition to these measures aimed at improving the efficiency of the Regional Co-operation System, the Governments considered it expedient to define a common regional position with respect to the principal political-environmental issues at both the regional and global levels, especially concerning multilateral negotiations and North-South relations relative to preparations for the United Nations Conference on Environment and Development to take place in Brazil in June 1992.

---

1. UNEP/LAC-IG.VI/6.

5. As a result, the Sixth Ministerial Meeting not only requested that an Action Plan be formulated to strengthen the Regional Co-operation System in environmental matters, but decided to conclude its discussions with the Declaration of Brasilia, which constitutes the theoretical and political basis of the Plan of Action.

6. The Action Plan, as an instrument designed by the region's Governments to strengthen regional co-operation in environmental matters, presupposes a common theoretical framework to comprehensively address the complex interrelations which exist between environmental problems and development concerns, at three different levels: national, regional and global. This comprehensive view should guide the implementation of the specific activities of the Action Plan at each of these different levels.

7. The Secretariat of UNEP was in charge of developing the Action Plan in collaboration with an Inter-Agency "core" group, made up of the Economic Commission for Latin America and the Caribbean (ECLAC), the Inter-American Development Bank (IDB) and the United Nations Development Programme (UNDP).

8. In drafting the document, special attention was given, as a political context for the Plan of Action, to the report "Our Own Agenda" prepared by the Commission on Development and Environment in Latin America and the Caribbean under the sponsorship of IDB and UNDP in collaboration with ECLAC and UNEP.

9. Extensive consultations were undertaken for the preparation of the Action Plan including an Informal Consultative Meeting of experts, who were invited in a personal capacity (Economic Commission for Latin America and the Caribbean headquarters in Santiago, Chile, February 1990); an Inter-Agency Meeting at the headquarters of the Latin American Economic System (SELA) (Caracas, Venezuela, March 1990); and a Meeting of High-level Experts Designated by Governments, convened by UNEP and hosted by the Government of Chile, 10–13 July 1990.

II. CONCEPTUAL FRAMEWORK

10. There is a clear consensus among the Governments that the impact of the foreign debt on the majority of the countries of the region has brought about a considerable contraction in national economies and a significant decrease in public expenditures, which in turn have caused an important reduction in the activities related to protecting and enhancing the environment.

11. This situation contradicts the opinions expressed by the

international community, especially developed countries, concerning the need for stronger national environmental policies to implement effective environmental management. It also places in doubt the feasibility of attaining the objectives of sustained development, as stated in the Report of the World Commission on Environment and Development entitled "Our Common Future"[2], and in the document "Environmental Perspective to the Year 2000 and Beyond"[3].

12. In this respect, the solution to the problem of the foreign debt and the creation of a New International Economic Order, which is both fair and equitable, are indispensable prerequisites to ensure democracy, security, peace and sustainable development in the region.

13. The natural heritage of the region, consisting of extremely valuable biological and mineral resources, has been contributing, during almost five centuries, to the development of the industrialized nations. The manner in which natural resources (mineral, forestry, fishery, wildlife, arable land and energy) have been exploited, as well as agricultural practices that did not take into account the unique characteristics of each ecosystem, have caused an environmental deterioration which is still going on at an increased pace. Therefore industrialized nations can be said to have a substantial environmental debt with Latin America and the Caribbean.

14. Our understanding of foreign debt should consequently be revised in light of a new ethical focus on economic and financial relations, which recognizes the concept of environmental debt.

15. There is an unbreakable bond between environmental deterioration and poverty. Both are parallel and interacting effects of a common global process of unbalanced growth. Improvement of economic and social conditions will be the determining factor in bringing to a halt the environmental degradation of the region.

16. It is equally important to strike a balance between development and the protection and preservation of the environment. To achieve this, it is necessary to promote a greater understanding of the nature and seriousness of environmental problems among planners and economic policymakers. Environmental protection must become an integral part of the economic, social and cultural development of the nations of the region.

17. The environment must be recognized as the planet's vital base, which includes Man and his relationship with natural resources—development as a process aimed at meeting human needs. Consequently, natural resource management, environmental policies and sustainable development

---

2. UNEP/GC.14/13.1987.
3. Official Document, AG/A42/25, Annex II. 1987.

should aim to improve the quality of life without degrading the environment, with Man maintaining or recovering the potential and well-being of all life on the planet as an integral part of nature, instead of something apart.

18. Protecting the environment and achieving sustainable development in the region should be the responsibility of the entire population of Latin America and the Caribbean. Environmental management is a task not just for the public sector, but for the entire community; the participation of all sectors of society is necessary.

19. In seeking solutions to regional, subregional and national environmental problems through the Action Plan for the Environment in Latin America and the Caribbean, recognition of different levels of development, different ecological conditions, different social and cultural considerations would require common activities to be tailored to local situations.

20. In the decade of the 1990s, implementation of environmental protection and enhancement projects in the countries of the region will depend basically on firm political commitment from the Governments of the region, supported by appropriate plans and financial resources. Funding will be possible through reallocation of national resources and, to a large extent, sufficient additional financial resources provided under concessional terms by the international community and its financial organizations.

21. International support could take the form of scientific information transfer, technical assistance, or financial aid, either directly to countries to support national activities, or through the Action Plan mechanism, to back up subregional and regional projects.

22. Access to scientific environmental protection information and technology at minimum cost is essential to facilitate the implementation of measures to control pollution from industrial sources and suitable management of the inputs and effluents of most production activities in the region, particularly in urban areas.

23. To effectively meet the global environmental challenges of the 1990s, international co-operation must reach new levels of concrete achievement. The active participation of all countries is essential to solve or attenuate the environmental problems threatening planetary stability, such as: the depletion of the ozone layer, climatic changes caused by pollution, the disposal of hazardous wastes and the loss of biodiversity. The Latin American and Caribbean region should take a firm stand on these global issues, participating actively in seeking their solution, without losing track of its particular regional perspective, i.e., to strive for fairer international pricing for its natural resources, which are a fundamental source of national income.

III. THE PRINCIPAL ENVIRONMENTAL PROBLEMS OF THE REGION, RESPONSES AND OBSTACLES THAT NEED TO BE OVERCOME, A BRIEF APPRAISAL

A. The Principal Problems

24. Accelerated economic and population growth in Latin America and the Caribbean[4], together with the development styles that have prevailed over the past five decades, gave rise to vast transformations in the fabric of society and its relationship to nature: the urban concentration of the population; the mushrooming of unplanned human settlements; the development of capital- and technology-intensive agriculture; the improvement of public health; the development of rapid communications and transport systems; greater economic integration; exponential growth of industry; the introduction into the environment of an enormous amount of new chemical compounds for agricultural, industrial and domestic uses; and the generation of impressive amounts of wastes.

25. The most common environmental deterioration mechanisms have been linked to the implementation of inappropriate production and technology strategies, unrelated to the diverse cultural and ecological contexts where they were applied and aimed at unsustainable maximization of benefits in the short term.

1. Resource management problems

• Deforestation

26. Over the past five years, deforestation in the region has risen at an average annual rate of almost 50,000 km^2. In the last 30 years, nearly 2 million km^2 of forests, an area greater than that of Mexico, have been lost. For the most part, those forestry resources were burnt. The effects of such deforestation are particularly devastating in the small island States of the Caribbean. In addition to being a regrettable loss of a valuable resource, regional burning of forests has accounted for up to 7 percent of the total world emissions of carbon dioxide, the main greenhouse gas responsible for global warming.

• Soil loss and degradation

27. Deforestation has intensified erosion processes. At the beginning of the 1980s, it was estimated that more than 2 million km^2, equivalent to

4. From 1950 to date, the population of the region has more than tripled, rising from 125 to 380 million inhabitants. During that same period, the GNP grew from 100 to 700 billion dollars and total annual energy consumption rose from 50 to 270 million tons of oil equivalents.

10 percent of the region's area, were already undergoing moderate to severe desertification.

28. The transformation of tropical forests into grazing land for extensive cattle raising and subsistence hillside farming is a predominant process in the region's rural areas and contributes to soil degradation. In the Amazonian subregion, it is estimated that one third of the land that has been converted into grazing land has become degraded. That ecological degradation, together with marketing problems, jeopardizes the viability of extensive livestock raising.

• The deterioration of marine and coastal resources

29. Mangrove, marshes, coastal lagoons and coral reefs, all particularly fragile ecosystems, have undergone degradation which is frequently irreversible through poorly planned development or pollution problems, with the consequent reduction in their fisheries potential. Marine resources and ocean ecosystems (including reefs and breeding areas) have been adversely affected by over-fishing, destructive fishing practices and inappropriate fishing technology; by oil spills and by the dumping of wastes. Beaches have also deteriorated through excessive and inappropriate use for recreation (including tourism), construction and sand mining.

• The deterioration of water resources

30. Nearly 80 percent of the region's urban population and 30 percent of its rural population have access to piped drinking water. Its quality is, however, a matter of growing concern.

31. In many urban areas, the disposal of liquid and solid municipal wastes is unsuitable and contributes to the deterioration of waterways, surface bodies of water and aquifers. Less than 5 percent of the municipal wastewater in Latin America and the Caribbean is treated prior to discharge.

2. Environmental quality problems

• The urban environmental predicament

32. In past decades, Latin American and Caribbean cities grew at rates unprecedented in the world. It is estimated that by the end of the present decade nearly 60 percent of the region's urban population will live in cities of more than 100,000 inhabitants and 30 percent in cities of more than 1 million inhabitants, with serious deficiencies in basic public services. Recent deterioration in the urban environment poses a serious public health problem. More than 50 million people are now exposed to hazardous levels of air pollution in the region's urban areas.

•   Environmental impacts of mining activities

33. Mining activities are also giving rise to serious, specific problems of deforestation, land degradation, and air and water pollution in different countries of the region.

•   Environmental consequences of energy issues

34. The economic processes of the region are not very efficient in the use of energy. This underscores the need for a stronger focus on energy conservation and greater emphasis on the development and application of alternate environmentally sustainable sources of energy.

35. The detrimental environmental impacts stemming from the harnessing of energy from a wide range of sources can be severe and irreversible. In some subregions overexploitation of fuelwood results in degraded watersheds; hydrocarbon exploration and exploitation can result in oil spills and the possible destruction of natural areas; large hydropower and thermoelectric projects can have adverse environmental impacts. The development of nuclear power plants raises new environmental concerns relative to potential accidents and the disposal of radioactive waste.

•   The extinction of native and folk cultures

36. Ethnic groups and indigenous communities whose survival is closely linked to the traditional uses of natural resources are now in serious danger of disappearing, because of both the change in habitats and the acculturation processes.

•   Illegal drug-crop cultivation

37. Drug trafficking corrupts society, distorts the economy and undermines the capacity of the Governments to manage their territory and production processes. The illegal production of drugs also affects the environment through deforestation, soil degradation and river pollution.

3. Global environmental problems

•   Climatic changes

38. The warming of the earth's atmosphere resulting from the accumulation of greenhouse gases is expected to induce climate changes that could include, among other things, modification of rainfall patterns and increases in the mean sea level. Possible regional effects of these processes are still uncertain, however they are potentially threatening, particularly to island and coastal States.

- Ozone layer depletion

39. The thinning of the protective ozone layer in the upper atmosphere, due to emissions of chlorofluorocarbons and other gases, increases the population's exposure to ultraviolet rays, resulting in harmful effects on health.

- Transboundary hazardous waste movements

40. Owing to stricter environmental controls being enforced in the industrialized countries, there is a growing trend to export hazardous wastes to the developing regions. Thus, the risk of receiving undesirable shipments in the region has increased, and the transit of such wastes, including radioactive wastes, through the seas of the region is extremely dangerous.

- Loss of biodiversity

41. It is now known that the biodiversity in Latin America and the Caribbean is unparalleled in other regions of the world. In 1980, natural protected areas covered only 350,000 km^2, less than 2 percent of the region's area. If the current rate of ecological destruction continues, it is estimated that between 100,000 and 350,000 species, scarcely known for the most part, could disappear over the next 40 years. This loss of biodiversity, comparable to the great cataclysmic extinctions of geological history, affects not only the region but humanity as a whole.

B. The Regional Response to Environmental Problems

42. Without underestimating some earlier though no less valuable initiatives[5], it may be stated that the United Nations Conference on the Human Environment, held in Stockholm in 1972, marked a qualitative leap in the regional response to urgent environmental problems. Since that time, public awareness has been strengthened and most of the Governments have established environmental institutions (ministries, undersecretariats and general directorates) and have enacted specific environmental legislation. The countries of the region have also expanded their international participation and have adopted subregional, regional or global environmental co-operation initiatives[6]. The region has also witnessed a growing involvement of non-governmental organizations in response to environmental problems.

5. Some international co-operation activities, such as the Convention on Nature Protection and Wildlife Preservation in the Western Hemisphere.
6. This appendix presents a summary of some of the most important international agree—ments for environmental protection suscribed in recent years by the regional governments.

43. Many subregions and subregional organizations have assumed growing environmental commitments, such as those mentioned below:

43.1. In the framework of the Treaty for Amazonian Co-operation (1978), a Special Commission for the Amazonian Environment (CEMAA) was established[7].

43.2. The Caribbean Community organized a Ministerial Conference on the Environment[8]. Other Caribbean countries participated in this Conference.

43.3. The Central American countries established a Central American Commission on Environment and Development[9].

43.4. The Andres Bello Agreement (1970) has developed environmental programmes in the field of science and technology.

43.5. With the support of UNEP, the coastal States of the Wider Caribbean and the South-East Pacific adopted Action Plans and international agreements for the management of their marine and coastal resources.

43.6. Through its Intergovernmental Co-ordinating Committee (CIC), the River Plate Basin Treaty (1969) promotes technical studies for the development of projects linked to optimum use of the Basin.

44. Regional Organizations, such as the Organization of American States (OAS), the Latin American Energy Organization (OLADE), the Latin American Economic System (SELA), the Inter-American Development Bank (IDB) and the agencies of the United Nations System have given impetus to a growing number of environmental activities, including the Tropical Forestry Action Plan (FAO/UNEP), which have been initiated in many of the countries throughout the region. UNDP and IDB have sponsored the formulation of an agenda for sustainable development in the region.

45. The First Intergovernmental Meeting on the Environment in Latin America and the Caribbean, convened by the Government of Mexico and

---

7. The environmental policy of the Treaty for Amazonian Co-operation was defined at the Third Meeting of Foreign Ministers (Quito, 6–8 March 1989). At that time, the Declaration of San Francisco de Quito, which includes the decision to establish the Special Commission for the Amazonian Environment, was signed. The Amazonian Declaration (Manaos, 6 May 1989) ratified those bases of the environmental policy. The first meeting of the Special Commission for the Amazonian Environment was held in Brasilia on November 1989, the second on May 1990, in Bogota, Colombia and the third one was held in Belem, Brazil, in January 1991.

8. The First Ministerial Conference on the Environment of CARICOM took place in Port-of-Spain, Trinidad and Tobago, from 31 May to 2 June 1989. The Port-of-Spain Accord on the Management and Conservation of the Caribbean Environment was signed at that Conference. The Second Ministerial Conference held in Kingston on September 10–11, 1990 continued the work to delineate the priorities and develop a programme of activities to address those priorities in the sub-region.

9. The decision to establish the Commission was taken in August 1989 in Guatemala.

UNEP in 1982, initiated a consultation process with government officials responsible for the environmental portfolio. At that meeting, the Governments agreed that the regional and subregional approach was most suitable to confront common environmental problems, and they requested UNEP, in consultation with the Governments, to formulate guidelines for the development of regional environmental programmes. Five subsequent intergovernmental meetings consolidated this consultative process, which resulted in the establishment of an *ad hoc* Regional System for Co-operation in Environmental Matters and the implementation of some specific regional programmes.

46. The Declaration of Brasilia, on whose principles the present Action Plan is based, was issued at the Sixth Ministerial Meeting on the Environment in Latin America and the Caribbean (Brasilia, 30–31 March 1989)[10.]

C. Obstacles to Environmental Management in Latin America and the Caribbean

47. In spite of the notable efforts described, the serious environmental problems of the region have generally tended to grow worse in recent years. Today, the concrete results of environmental management fall far below the degree of awareness acquired.

48. Among the numerous factors that reduce the effectiveness of environmental management, the following are critical:

48.1. Persistence of adverse environmental effects in the region as a result of the current international economic order.

48.2. Insufficient funding and lack of co-ordination. The absence of effective exchange of information and co-ordination among the numerous organizations and institutions that promote environmental activities in the region causes duplication of efforts.

48.3. Insufficient conceptual and institutional bases for full incorporation of the environmental dimension in development planning and insufficient environmental assessment of development projects.

48.4. The prevalence of sectorial approaches incompatible with the transdisciplinary nature of environmental problems.

48.5. Insufficient and unstructured environmental information, which lacks bases for comparison.

48.6. The influence of the economic crisis of the 1980s, which has relegated environmental matters to a low level of priority.

48.7. Insufficient research on environmental problems. The

---

10. UNEP/LAC-IG.VI/6.

scientific institutions of the region have felt the effects of the crisis with particular intensity.

48.8. The lack of concern within the technical agencies of several countries to effectively incorporate environmental education within the different levels of formal and non-formal national education programmes, as well as the lack of adequate incentives, at both sub-regional and regional levels, to promote this educational approach.

48.9. The ideological or cultural predominance of destructive technologies.

48.10. The lack of effective measures by industrialized countries to address global problems for which they are chiefly responsible.

48.11. The development strategies pursued by the countries of the region have not given enough consideration to the limited and exhaustible nature of environmental resources.

48.12. The noticeable tendency among industrialized countries to use environmental arguments to block access of the region's exports to their markets. In this regard, the application of non-tariff barriers, based on environmental factors, which affect the growth potential of Latin America and the Caribbean, must be rejected.

IV. THE OBJECTIVES OF THE ACTION PLAN

49. The principle objective of the Action Plan is to strengthen the capacity for political decision-making and action to streamline the Regional Co-operation System on the Environment in Latin America and the Caribbean, the goals of which have been defined by Governments[11] as follows:

49.1. To promote the sustainable use of the vast natural wealth of the region for the economic and social development of its peoples and improve their quality of life.

49.2. To turn about the trends that are impoverishing the resource base of the region.

49.3. To establish the foundations for the initiation of sustainable development processes within each of the countries of the region.

49.4. To establish a common regional position vis-à-vis global and regional environmental issues.

49.5. To stimulate horizontal regional co-operation on environmental matters to help support national environmental management initiatives.

49.6. To encourage the maintenance of a satisfactory level of

---

11. UNEP/IG.40/7; UNEP/IG.57/8; UNEP/IG.76/4; UNEP/LAC-IG.VI/6.

environmental quality in all urban areas, and industrial and rural communities through the use of appropriate environmental standards and the deployment of environmental protection and control measures.

50. To attain these general objectives, the Action Plan seeks concrete objectives at the national, regional and global levels, as follows:

National Level

51. The strengthening of environmental administrations in each of the countries of the region, the formulation of national environmental policies, the development of environmental legislation, the establishment of interinstitutional co-ordination mechanisms within the country, the promotion of environmental education and awareness campaigns, and other activities designed to safeguard the environment.

Regional Level

52. Enhancement of regional co-operation through: more effective co-ordination and information exchange mechanisms, continuity between intergovernmental meetings, implementation of regional agreements, co-ordination and linkage of the environmental initiatives undertaken in the region, formulation and implementation of regional and subregional projects, effective monitoring, evaluation of the Regional Co-operation System activities, and the establishment of new institutional provisions for the aforementioned purposes. The Action Plan gives full recognition to the sub-regional programmes and the existing institutional arrangements which shall be eligible for support from resources mobilized by the Action Plan.

Global Level

53. Greater involvement in global issues, given their regional implications; more active participation of the region's Governments in programming UNEP's activities and budget; the development of international environmental legislation; the strengthening of a regional policy position in the multilateral negotiations preparatory to the United Nations Conference on Environment and Development, to be held in Brazil in 1992, as well as during the Conference[12].

---

12. Resolution 44/228, United Nations General Assembly.

V. THE STRATEGIC COMPONENT OF THE PLAN

54. The common environmental, economic and social problems shared by the region of Latin America and the Caribbean, as well as the peculiar characteristics of the subregions that comprise it, make it necessary to assign priority to the regional and subregional activities and projects included, as a basic strategy for the Plan.

55. The strategic principles of the Action Plan are:

55.1. To encourage subregional policies, plans, programmes, and projects whose goals are aimed at environmental planning and management of production activities in the territory of the subregions in their ecological, economic and social contexts; and to support the Governments that comprise the subregions in adopting measures and decisions for their implementation and followup.

55.2. To support subregional agreements that will promote the implementation of productive and development projects that are comprehensively and sustainably planned, using instruments such as environmental impact assessment (EIA) and risk analysis, so that maximum efficiency and effectiveness may be achieved in terms of time, cost and political acceptance.

55.3. To encourage harmonization of the environmental legislation and regulations of the various countries of the region and to support related horizontal co-operation between the countries. This would allow for more effective co-operation in solving common environmental problems and in achieving environmental planning and management goals for the region.

55.4. To support regional and subregional studies to identify probable causes of environmental imbalances and their relationship to production projects, and to stimulate the implementation of joint activities for monitoring, follow-up, information exchange and the preparation of rehabilitation projects.

55.5. To give priority to preventive environmental protection activities in the region, thereby making better use of the economic resources allocated and avoiding the higher cost involved in correcting environmental impacts, even when scientific evidence of such impacts is not conclusive.

55.6. To support the environmental training and education of human resources, as a basis for effective action by Governments; and promote, at every level, the environmental education of the population, as the basis of civic responsibility and participation.

55.7. To promote greater citizen awareness, particularly through non-governmental organizations, and encourage responsible citizen participation in solving environmental problems.

55.8. To provide incentives for national and regional scientific research and horizontal transfer of technology, develop appropriate and clean methods of production, and replace all types of harmful technologies.

55.9. To identify and protect, in an appropriate way, the flora and fauna, as well as national and regional ecosystems in a manner compatible with the sustainable use of resources, the preservation of biological diversity and the conservation of designated spaces, which comprise the biological, geographical, scenic and cultural heritage of the countries of the region.

55.10. To protect the region by prohibiting, under any circumstances, the entry of all types of hazardous, toxic, harmful and radioactive wastes; and to put into operation regional monitoring and control mechanisms for the safe transport, treatment and disposal of wastes produced within the region. In the case of radioactive wastes, to ensure compliance with the guidelines established by the International Atomic Energy Agency (IAEA).

55.11. To reach agreement with the international agencies on the co-ordination of their environmental activities in the region, thereby providing effective, unified and concurrent support, and avoiding the scattering and duplication of efforts on similar issues.

55.12. To seek an adequate response and commitment by the industrialized countries to assist the region in addressing its environmental problems, many of which have their genesis in and are sustained by actions of the industrialized community.

56. The political will and unified commitment of the Governments of the region in the planning and implementation of common solutions to its economic, social and environmental problems is the strategic key for the implementation of this Action Plan. Moreover, the will and commitment of the international agencies to concurrent and co-ordinated action in support of the Action Plan are also strategic keys to its success.

VI. THE PROGRAMME COMPONENT

57. Table 1 presents the programme elements that are proposed as an integral part of the Action Plan. These include ongoing programmes and new priority programmes addressing subregional, regional and global environmental problems, as determined by the Governments of the region[13].

---

13. UNEP/LAC-IG.VI/6; UNEP/LAC.IEG.1/6.

58. In its initial phase the Action Plan's activities will focus on the strengthening of ongoing programmes:

58.1.   Regional Programme for planning development and environment (PR-3);
58.2.   Regional Programme on environmental legislation and institutional framework (PR-5);
58.3.   Regional Programme on environmental education (PR-6);
58.4.   Regional Programme on protection and conservation of the natural and cultural heritage and of protected areas (PR-10);
58.5.   Regional Environmental Training Network;
58.6.   Action Plan for the South-East Pacific; and
58.7.   Action Plan for the Caribbean Environment Programme.

and the initiation of new basic regional support programmes:

58.8.   Management of national and multi-national watersheds;
58.9.   Regional Environmental Information Service;
58.10. Programme to promote the transfer and adaptation of environmental protection technologies; and
58.11. Programme to strengthen environmental management organizations in Latin America and the Caribbean.

59. As resources become available, activities will also be initiated within the other programme areas indicated in Table 1.

A. Implementation of the Programmes

60. Successful implementation of the programmes will depend to a large extent on the gradual evolution of well designed co-operation projects that result in concrete benefits for the participating Governments.

61. The above programmes will be implemented by means of specific projects and activities to be decided upon by the Governments with the technical assistance of the Secretariat, in consultation with international, regional, and subregional organizations.

62. For the development of the specific regional co-operative projects, the following steps will be undertaken during the first phase of the Plan's implementation:

62.1. Thematic joint programming exercises with international and regional organizations to assess ongoing activities within each programme element.

Table 1 Programming Areas of the Action Plan

Environmental Management and Institutional Development

Programmes	Objectives
I. Regional Information Exchange Service**	Establish a computer network for the exchange of information among individuals and groups and for access to data bases on the environment
II. Environmental Training Network*	Design and co-ordinate environmental education and training processes in the region
III. Institutional Strengthening and Citizen Participation**	Strengthen environmental institutions and promote the participation of non-governmental sectors in solving environmental problems
IV. Development of Policies and Legislation (PR-5)*	Promote the formulation of environmental policies and their legal and institutional framework
V. Development Planning and Environment (PR-3)*	Incorporate environmental criteria into development planning and develop guidelines for environmental impact assessment
VI. Environmental Education (PR-6)*	Increase environmental awareness in the region, incorporating environmental elements into formal and informal education programmes (mass media)

Resource Management

Programmes	Objectives
I. Management and Planning of Natural Resources in Rural Areas	Determine optimal land-use patterns for the utilization of resources in rural areas of the region
II. Environmental Management and Development Control in Urban Areas	Determine the land-use controls to mitigate the adverse environmental impacts of urban processes in the region
III. Environmental Management and Development Control in Island Territories	Determine the land-use controls to mitigate the adverse environmental impacts of development processes in island territories
IV. Protection of Natural Areas and Cultural Heritage (PR-10)*	Administer protected areas and endangered species; implement the world conservation strategies
V. Management of Tropical and Subtropical Forests*	Promote sustainable utilization of tropical and subtropical forests
VI. Extension of Tropical and Sub-Tropical Forest Areas by Reforestation with Preferably Native Species	Enhance the contribution of the tropical and sub-tropical forest formations to global climate amelioration

(continues)

Table 1 (*continued*)

Programmes	Objectives
VII. Conservation of Biodiversity	Conduct integrated conservation programmes, scientific taxonomic studies, studies to identify the potential economic value of biodiversity, and formulate pilot projects for its utilization
VIII. Control and Restoration of Altered Ecosystems	Identify the most degraded areas in the region and formulate control and remedial measures
IX. Low-Input Sustainable Agriculture	Achieve an optimal mix of inputs in agricultural production that would minimize the adverse impacts on the environment
X. Environmental Impact on Marine and Coastal Ecosystems	Determine the economic implications of coastal environmental degradation and formulate prevention and restoration strategies
XI. Management of National and Multinational Watersheds**	Plan the utilization of national watershed and promote co-operative programmes for multinational river basins
XII. Subregional Seas*	Protect the marine and coastal environments of the South-East Pacific and the Wider Caribbean subregions
XIII. Population, Resources, Environment and Development	Design comprehensive plans for sustainable development that take fully into account the singular and combined effects of population resource utilization, environment and development; promote indigenous technologies and the participation of native groups
XIV. Co-Operation to Face Natural Disasters and Mitigation of the Environmental Effects	Minimize the adverse effects of natural disasters, such as floods, hurricanes, landslides, volcanic eruptions and other seismic events
XV. Wetlands Management	Identify and assess the potential of marine and freshwater wetlands for sustainable development
XVI. Desertification Control	Identify the physical and biological processes contributing to desertification and monitor the progression of this phenomenon
XVII. Protected Area Management	Identify, classify and manage areas meeting the criteria established for the designation of protected areas
XVIII. Management of Highland Ecosystems	Manage highland ecosystems based on principles of sustainable development

(*continues*)

Table 1 (*continued*)

	Programmes	Objectives
XIX.	Design of Geographical Information System (GIS) for Environmental Management and Development Planning	Use of GIS in the environmental management decisionmaking process

Pollution Prevention and Control

	Programmes	Objectives
I.	Management of Wastewater and Solid Waste	Identify viable alternatives for urban and industrial waste management in the countries of the region
II.	Prevention and Control of Air Pollution	Determine suitable cost-effective strategies to combat air pollution in the metropolitan and industrial areas of the region
III.	Prevention and Control of Water Pollution	Formulate effective strategies to monitor and protect the quality of water resources
IV.	Life Cycle Management of Toxic Residues and Hazardous Chemicals	Identify critical areas in the region where the management of toxic residues and the production and use of chemicals present a potential public hazard, and formulate suitable life cycle management policies
V.	Saving and Efficient Use of Existing and Alternative Energy Sources	Rationalize the utilization of fuels, reduce the adverse environmental effects of their production and consumption, and identify suitable alternative energy sources
VI.	Transfer and Adaptation of Environmental Protection Technologies**	Provide practical and cost-effective technologies for air and water quality management and pollution control, appropriate to the Latin American and Caribbean countries

Global Environmental Problems

	Programmes	Objectives
I.	Development of Regional Positions on Climatic Change, Depletion of the Ozone Layer, Conservation of Biodiversity, and Management of Hazardous Wastes	Strengthen the Governments' capacity to identify the impact of global environmental issues and participate in global efforts aimed at solving the different problems

*Programmes under way.
**New programmes of special priority.

62.2. Identification of projects that could be launched to supplement existing efforts and fill in gaps.

62.3. Programming exercises with national institutions selected for the implementation of projects or activities.

62.4. Procurement of financial support on a case-by-case basis, seeking funds for each specific project from multiple sources; Governments, bilateral and multilateral organizations and the United Nations System.

62.5. Establishment of effective mechanisms for timely and detailed evaluation of the Action Plan as a whole and of its programmes and projects.

B. Contribution of the Programmes to the Strengthening of Regional Co-operation

63. The integrated approach to programme implementation of the Action plan not only will yield specific results out of each project, but will also produce the following spin-off outputs:

63.1. Avoid duplication of institutional and personnel resources by making maximum use of horizontal regional co-operation;

63.2. Incorporate the sustainable development concept in all programmes and projects;

63.3. Strengthen the consultation and information exchange process between intergovernmental organizations, agencies and programmes of the United Nations System, bilateral and multilateral funding agencies, and non-governmental organizations to prevent duplication and to take advantage of complementarity in project activities;

63.4. Reinforce regional horizontal co-operation to buttress regional capabilities, and substantively increase the region's self-support in priority environmental matters; and

63.5. Strengthen national institutions and encourage their active involvement in the formulation and implementation of environmental protection and improvement policies.

VII. INSTITUTIONAL ARRANGEMENTS

64. Implementation of the Action Plan will require institutional instruments to promote it, to follow up intergovernmental decisions, to monitor programme development and to administer co-ordination mechanisms. These instruments are: ministerial meetings, intersessional

policy body, national focal points, secretariat of the action plan, inter-agency consultative support group, and *ad hoc* scientific advisory groups.

Ministerial Meetings on the Environment

65. The Ministerial Meetings on the Environment shall constitute the General Authority of the Action Plan and the other institutional instruments provided for shall serve as its auxiliaries. The maximum environmental authorities of the Governments of the region shall participate in these meetings and shall be empowered to establish priorities and assess, approve or review the Action Plan. These meetings shall be held every two years at least six months prior to the related session of the UNEP Governing Council. The host country, assisted by the Secretariat of the Action Plan, shall be responsible for convening the Ministerial Meetings and providing them with the support required.

Inter-Sessional Policy Body

66. The Inter-Sessional Policy Body shall be formed by the seven Member States that have served as officers at the preceding Ministerial Meeting and shall be open to all Member States of Latin America and the Caribbean. The policy orientation functions of the Action Plan shall fall on this Body during the inter-sessional periods of Ministerial Meetings.

67. The functions of the Inter-Sessional Policy Body shall be:

67.1. To advise the Secretariat in fulfilling the guidelines approved.

67.2. To promote the active participation of all the countries of the region in the Action Plan.

67.3. To assist in obtaining funds for the Action Plan activities.

67.4. To formulate the rules of procedure required to suitably carry out the activities linked to the Action Plan.

67.5. To provide the Secretariat with directives for the preparation of the agenda for the subsequent Ministerial Meeting.

National Focal Points

68. Each of the Governments participating in the Action Plan shall designate an institution to act as a National Focal Point through which activities and communications related to the Plan shall be channelled.

69. The functions of the National Focal Point shall be:

69.1. To promote the broadest participation of national

institutions in the activities of the Action Plan, so that environmental problems are formulated from concerted multisectorial approaches.

69.2. To designate national scientific and technical or management institutions to be in charge of implementing the different regional or subregional projects implemented within the framework of the Action Plan.

69.3. To follow up on all activities conducted in the country in relation to the Plan and to serve as a liaison with the Secretariat of the Action Plan.

The Secretariat of the Action Plan

70. The overall functions of the Secretariat shall be to co-ordinate the activities of the Action Plan, and specifically to:

70.1. Provide the national and international institutions participating in the implementation of the Plan with technical support and guidance, information and co-ordination facilities.

70.2. Prepare, in consultation with the National Focal Points and the Inter-Sessional Policy Body, as well as relevant national and international institutions, the project proposals to implement the programmes agreed on.

70.3. Promote fund-raising to finance the projects and activities approved.

70.4. Prepare progress reports on programmes and projects under way and present them to the Ministerial Meetings.

70.5. Prepare, in consultation with the Inter-Sessional Policy Body, the agenda and documents for the Ministerial Meetings.

70.6. Evaluate and monitor project implementation together with the National Focal Points.

70.7. Propose to international agencies and to participating regional and subregional bodies that they adopt standard methodologies and formats to make data compatible.

71. One of the main functions of the Secretariat shall be to implement the Regional Information Exchange Programme. This information exchange system will facilitate monitoring the progress of the Action Plan projects through an electronic communications network between national and international institutions undertaking environmental actions in the region.

72. In all matters falling within the sphere of its functions, the Secretariat shall work in close contact with the secretariats of existing regional and subregional environmental programmes, such as the Environmental Training Network, the Action Plans for the Wider Caribbean and the South-East Pacific, the Treaty for Amazonian Co-operation, the

CARICOM Consultative Group on the Environment, the Treaty of the River Plate Basin and the Central American Commission on Environment and Development.

Inter-Agency Consultative Support Group

73. The Inter-Agency Consultative Support Group shall be composed of representatives of agencies and programmes of the United Nations System, the Inter-American System, regional and subregional intergovernmental bodies, bilateral or multilateral development support institutions and non-governmental organizations. On the basis of a proposal of the Secretariat, the Inter-Sessional Policy Body shall determine the specific composition of this Inter-Agency Consultative Support Group, which the Secretariat itself shall be in charge of convening on an *ad hoc* basis.

74. The principal functions of the Inter-Agency Consultative Support Group shall be:

74.1. To collaborate with the Secretariat in reviewing projects and activities approved by the Ministerial Meetings and to co-ordinate its possible participation in them.

74.2. To provide the Secretariat with information on activities sponsored by the bodies represented when the activities may have an influence on environmental matters.

74.3. To assist the Secretariat and the Inter-Sessional Policy Body in their fund-raising activities.

74.4. To assist the Secretariat in preparing, at the request of the National Focal Points, joint inter-Agency consultative missions to assess, with the national counterpart sectors, key national environmental issues, formulate concerted programmes to address them, and identify co-operation opportunities with other countries.

Ad Hoc Scientific Advisory Groups

75. The *Ad hoc* Scientific Advisory Groups shall be composed of experts of the region of recognized national and international prestige, to be identified by the National Focal Points, and shall be called upon on an *ad hoc* and case-by-case basis to provide scientific advice to the Secretariat on:

75.1. The formulation and implementation of projects and programmes.

75.2. The assessment of critical regional and global environmental issues.

76. The institutional structure of the Action Plan appears in Figure 1.

Figure 1 Functional Flows for the Implementation of the Action Plan for
Environment in Latin America and the Caribbean

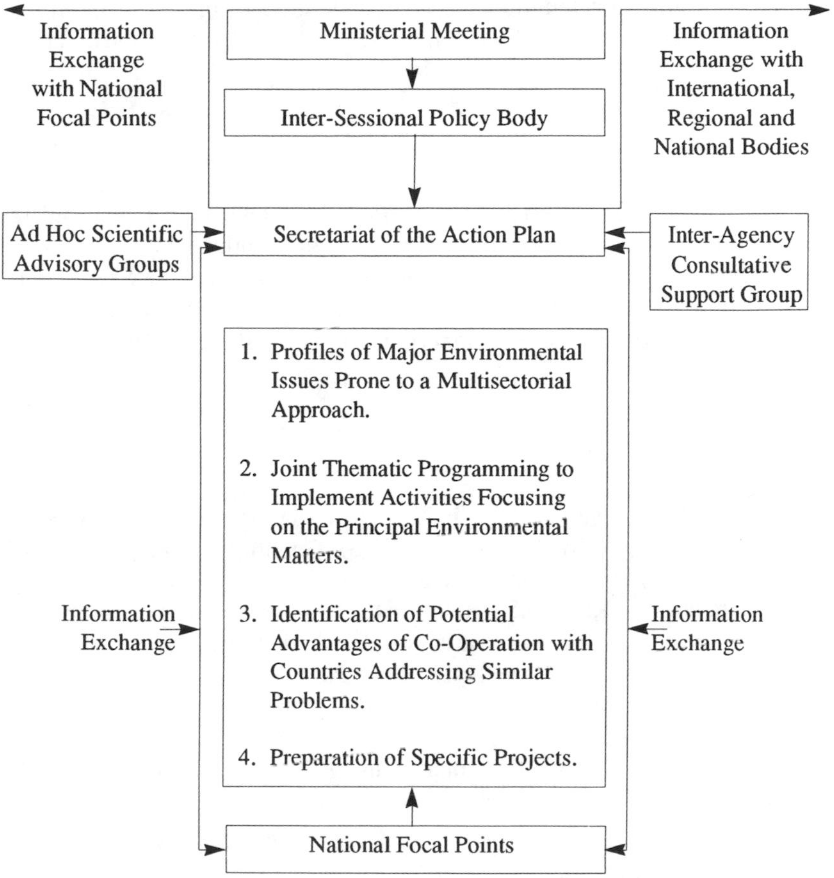

```
←────────────────────────────────────────────────────────────────────→
┌──────────────┐    ┌─────────────────────────┐    ┌──────────────┐
│ Information   │    │   Ministerial Meeting   │    │ Information   │
│ Exchange      │    └─────────────┬───────────┘    │ Exchange with │
│ with National │    ┌─────────────▼───────────┐    │ International,│
│ Focal Points  │    │ Inter-Sessional Policy Body│  │ Regional and  │
│               │    └─────────────┬───────────┘    │ National Bodies│
└──────────────┘                   │                └──────────────┘
┌──────────────┐    ┌─────────────▼───────────┐    ┌──────────────┐
│ Ad Hoc Scientific│→│ Secretariat of the Action Plan │←│ Inter-Agency  │
│ Advisory Groups  │ └─────────────────────────┘    │ Consultative  │
└──────────────┘                                     │ Support Group │
                                                      └──────────────┘
```

1. Profiles of Major Environmental Issues Prone to a Multisectorial Approach.

2. Joint Thematic Programming to Implement Activities Focusing on the Principal Environmental Matters.

Information Exchange →   3. Identification of Potential Advantages of Co-Operation with Countries Addressing Similar Problems.   ← Information Exchange

4. Preparation of Specific Projects.

National Focal Points

VIII. FINANCIAL ARRANGEMENTS

77. An essential prerequisite to attaining the objectives of the Action Plan is to secure additional financial support commensurate with the number of the regional and subregional projects that will need to be implemented in the 1990s. Sources could include the Governments themselves, as well as bilateral, multilateral and private sector assistance.

78. Additional financial resources are necessary to support the co-

ordination activities and the implementation of the Action Plan's subregional and regional projects.

79. The financial requirements are subdivided according to the three levels of implementation of the Plan: policy formulation, co-ordination mechanisms, and project implementation.

Policy Formulation

80. Policy formulation for the Action Plan shall take place during the regional ministerial meetings. These should continue to be financed by the convening Governments with the support of UNEP as Secretariat. Each country should provide financing for its representatives to the ministerial meetings and the meetings of the Inter-Sessional Policy Body.

Co-Ordination Mechanisms

81. UNEP will support the initial co-ordination of the Action Plan (1991–1993), subject to the approval of its Governing Council and the availability of funds in the Environment Fund. Its contributions will consist of strengthening its Regional Office for Latin America and the Caribbean (ROLAC) to act as the Secretariat of the Action Plan as well as the Ministerial Meetings and the Inter-Sessional Policy Body. Initially the strengthening of ROLAC will consist of two additional professionals and two support staff members.

82. The activities of the Inter-Agency Support Group should be financed by each of the participating agencies.

Project Implementation

83. Regional and subregional projects are the raison d'être of the Action Plan. The possible financial sources to support their implementation are:

- Regional and extraregional Governments;
- UNEP's Environment Fund;
- Multilateral funding organizations;
- International organizations;
- National technical co-operation and development agencies;
- Private foundations and non-governmental organizations.

84. Two mechanisms will be considered to secure the financial support of projects:

84.1. Handling each project case by case, according to the particular requirements and conditions of each funding agency.

84.2. Establishing a special account for environmental projects, with funds principally from sources outside the region, administered by a competent multilateral funding agency.

85. The Governments of the region should continue to fulfill and expand their commitments to existing programmes such as the Caribbean and South-East Pacific Action Plans and the Environmental Training Network.

a. Start-up Phase (1991–1993)

86. It is expected that after the Seventh Ministerial Meeting, all programme elements approved for implementation within the Action Plan would be incorporated by UNEP into the 1992–1993 Programme and Budget Document that would be presented to the sixteenth session of the Governing Council (May 1991) for consideration and approval.

87. Some of the priority actions of the Plan will therefore be initially supported by the UNEP Fund, subject to resource availability. For the implementation of a significant number of projects in the priority areas identified by Governments, substantial additional resources from Governments and other sources would be required.

88. It is proposed that a special ministerial-level meeting be held towards the end of 1991. The objectives would be to:

88.1. Approve the project proposals to implement the priority programmes of the Action Plan, which, in turn, would be submitted to funding agencies; and

88.2. Review a study prepared by the Secretariat concerning possible financial mechanisms at the national, subregional and regional levels to support the Action Plan. These financial mechanisms would be brought to the 1992 Conference through the Preparatory Committee.

89. This special meeting would be convened by UNEP. All potential funding sources would be invited to participate.

b. Full-Implementation Phase (1993 onwards)

90. During this phase it is expected that activities will be launched in all priority programme areas depending on the success of the fund-raising campaigns initiated during the first phase.

91. The preparation of project proposals to be initiated during the second phase of Action Plan implementation would be developed in the period between the special meeting referred to above and the Eighth Ministerial Meeting to be held towards the end of 1992.

92. This task would be carried out by the Secretariat through consultations and joint programming with regional bodies and international agencies, as well as with national institutions responsible for project implementation.

93. The project proposals would be submitted to the Eighth Ministerial Meeting for consideration and approval, and implementation would begin from 1993 onwards.

94. According to this schedule the programmes of the full-scale Action Plan would be incorporated in UNEP's 1994–1995 Programme and Budget Document to be considered at the seventeenth session of the Governing Council (May 1993).

95. Furthermore the Secretariat would adopt the necessary measures to incorporate the Action Plan programmes in the next exercise to formulate the System-Wide Medium-Term Plan on the Environment (1996–2001).

96. Figure 2 presents a flow diagram indicating the linkages between all the foreseen steps in the implementation of the various phases of the Action Plan.

APPENDIX

Examples of sub-regional, regional, and global international agreements on environmental protection subscribed by the governments of Latin America and the Caribbean:

- Convention on Nature Protection and Wildlife Preservation in the Western Hemisphere (Washington, 1940).
- Treaty of the River Plate Basin (Brasilia, 1969).
- Convention on the Protection of the Archaeological, Historical, and Artistic Heritage of the American Nations, also called Convention of San Salvador (Santiago de Chile, 1976).
- Treaty for Amazonian Cooperation (Brasilia, 1978).
- Convention for the Conservation and Management of the Vicuña (Lima, 1979).
- Convention on the Conservation of Antarctic Marine Living Resources (Canberra, 1980).
- Convention for the Protection of the Marine Environment and Coastal Areas of the South-East Pacific (Lima, 1981).
- Agreement on Regional Co-operation in Combatting Pollution on the South-East Pacific by Oil and Other Harmful Substances in Case of Emergencies (Lima, 1981). Supplementary Protocol to the Agreement (Quito, 1983).

Figure 2 Timetable of Plan's Activites and Their Links

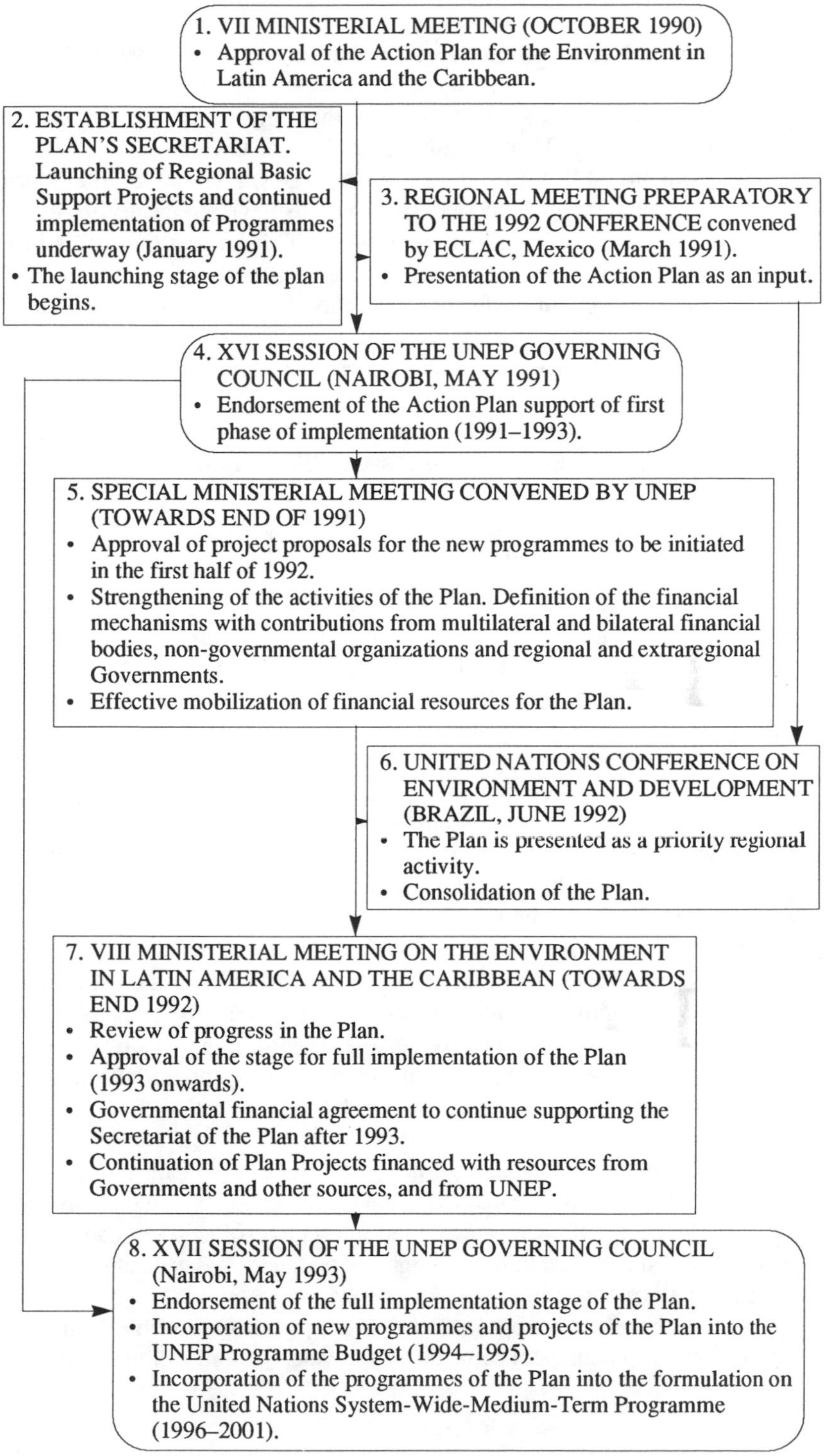

1. VII MINISTERIAL MEETING (OCTOBER 1990)
- Approval of the Action Plan for the Environment in Latin America and the Caribbean.

2. ESTABLISHMENT OF THE PLAN'S SECRETARIAT.
Launching of Regional Basic Support Projects and continued implementation of Programmes underway (January 1991).
- The launching stage of the plan begins.

3. REGIONAL MEETING PREPARATORY TO THE 1992 CONFERENCE convened by ECLAC, Mexico (March 1991).
- Presentation of the Action Plan as an input.

4. XVI SESSION OF THE UNEP GOVERNING COUNCIL (NAIROBI, MAY 1991)
- Endorsement of the Action Plan support of first phase of implementation (1991–1993).

5. SPECIAL MINISTERIAL MEETING CONVENED BY UNEP (TOWARDS END OF 1991)
- Approval of project proposals for the new programmes to be initiated in the first half of 1992.
- Strengthening of the activities of the Plan. Definition of the financial mechanisms with contributions from multilateral and bilateral financial bodies, non-governmental organizations and regional and extraregional Governments.
- Effective mobilization of financial resources for the Plan.

6. UNITED NATIONS CONFERENCE ON ENVIRONMENT AND DEVELOPMENT (BRAZIL, JUNE 1992)
- The Plan is presented as a priority regional activity.
- Consolidation of the Plan.

7. VIII MINISTERIAL MEETING ON THE ENVIRONMENT IN LATIN AMERICA AND THE CARIBBEAN (TOWARDS END 1992)
- Review of progress in the Plan.
- Approval of the stage for full implementation of the Plan (1993 onwards).
- Governmental financial agreement to continue supporting the Secretariat of the Plan after 1993.
- Continuation of Plan Projects financed with resources from Governments and other sources, and from UNEP.

8. XVII SESSION OF THE UNEP GOVERNING COUNCIL (Nairobi, May 1993)
- Endorsement of the full implementation stage of the Plan.
- Incorporation of new programmes and projects of the Plan into the UNEP Programme Budget (1994–1995).
- Incorporation of the programmes of the Plan into the formulation on the United Nations System-Wide-Medium-Term Programme (1996–2001).

- United Nations Convention on the Law of the Sea (Montego Bay, 1982).
- Protocol for the Protection of the South-East Pacific Against Pollution from Land-based Sources (Quito, 1983).
- Convention for the Protection and Development of the Marine Environment of the Wider Caribbean Region (Cartagena, 1983).
- Protocol Concerning Co-operation in Combatting Oil Spills in the Wider Caribbean Region (Cartagena, 1983).
- Vienna Convention for the Protection of the Ozone Layer (Vienna, 1985).
- Montreal Protocol on Substances that Deplete the Ozone Layer (Montreal, 1987).
- Basel Convention on the Control of Transboundary Movements of Hazardous Wastes and their Disposal (Basel, 1989).

A CALL TO ACTION

The Ministers and Representatives of countries participating in the VII Ministerial meeting on the Environment in Latin America and the Caribbean held in Port-of-Spain, 22–23 October, 1990, decided to conclude their deliberations with a call to action.

1. The VII Ministerial Meeting reaffirms the Declaration of Brasilia and reiterates the conviction that an adequate response to environmental challenges requires an unprecedented level of cooperation among countries and between regions of the world. Towards this end, and in the context of the Declaration of Brasilia, the countries participating in this Meeting approved an Action Plan for the Environment in Latin America and the Caribbean.

2. The Plan contains programmes aimed at arresting the deterioration of the environment, and for the recovery and rehabilitation of natural resources. It is also a framework for discharging regional obligations, to stabilize the ecological systems of Planet Earth and to minimize the disequilibria caused by the manner in which humanity acts with respect to the Earth's resources, which it holds in trust.

3. The Meeting considered that, given the complex inter-relationship between society and nature and the inseparable linkage between environment and development, the tasks and their respective objectives can only be undertaken and achieved through enlightened attitudes and dedicated efforts on the part of all sectors within any community.

4. The Meeting recognized the strong inter-relationship that exists between environmental concerns and the development model that prevails in

the world, and of the possible impacts of global environmental negotiations on the political and economic reality of the region.

5. The Meeting noted that recognition of mutual vulnerability to impacts of global changes has led to a number of important conventions, protocols, treaties, memoranda, agreements among varying groups of countries, each instrument setting out a normative framework based on the broad philosophical, political and practical concerns which underpin any issue. Although the Action Plan for the Environment for Latin America and the Caribbean takes its place among these, in essence, it represents a call to regional unity and action.

6. The Ministers expressed concern for the approach and treatment of the developed countries regarding environmental and economic topics, which results in new conditionalities for development financing.

7. One concern of Ministers attending this Meeting is the need to apply the principles of equity and social justice in the enjoyment of the product of the Earth's resources.

8. The Ministers consider the Action Plan which they have adopted at this Meeting to be a key mechanism for the preparation and presentation of the views and positions of this region at the United Nations Conference on Environment and Development, scheduled for June 1992 in Brazil.

9. On the basis of the above considerations, Ministers attending this VII Ministerial Meeting on the Environment in Latin America and the Caribbean issue this call to action:

- We commit ourselves to promote the Plan at the highest possible level, and to establish arrangements for extensive consultations and widespread participation among our people.
- We reaffirm our commitment to hemispheric solidarity, to the regional cooperation system and the promotion of the Action Plan for the Environment in Latin America and the Caribbean as an important instrument for strengthening such cooperation.
- We accept the Action Plan as a strategic document which must be a critical input into the regional preparatory arrangements leading to the United Nations Conference on Environment and Development, to be held in Brazil during 1992.
- We urge the international community, particularly the developed countries and the multilateral and bilateral financial and technical assistance institutions, to recognize that the Action Plan represents a framework for environmental management in Latin America and the Caribbean and that the programmes, projects and activities developed from it reflect the will of the countries of the region.

Port-of-Spain, Trinidad and Tobago
October 23, 1990

Simon Henderson
Minister in the Ministry of Finance,
    Ministry of Economic
    Development, Planning and
    Energy, Antigua and Barbuda

Alberto Barbuto
Presidente (Subsecretario de Estado),
    Comisión Nacional de Política
    Ambiental, Argentina

Glenn Livingston Archer
Director, Department of
    Environment Health, Ministry of
    Health, Bahamas

N. K. Simmons
Minister of Environment, Ministry
    of Employment, Labour
    Relations and Community
    Development, Barbados

Victor Gonzalez
Chief Environment Officer, Ministry
    of Tourism and the Environment,
    Belize

José Antonio Lutzenberger
Secretary, Secretary for the
    Environment Presidency of the
    Republic, Brazil

Luis Alvarado
Ministro, Ministerio de Bienes
    Nacionales, Chile

Helenio Ferrer Gracia
Vicepresidente, Comisión Nacional
    de Protección del Medio Ambiente
    y Conservación de los Recursos
    Naturales (COMARNA), Cuba

Eliud T. Williams
Permanent Secretary, Ministry of
    Agriculture, Dominica

Carlos Luzuriaga
Subsecretario de Medio Ambiente,
    Ministerio de Energia y Minas,
    Ecuador

Kenny Lalsingh
Minister, Ministry of Health,
    Environment, Community
    Development and
    Co-operatives, Grenada

Germán I. Rodríguez Arana
Director de Educación Ambiental
    Comisión Nacional del Medio
    Ambiente, Presidencia de la
    República, Guatemala

Walter A. Chin
Head, Guyana Agency for Health
    Sciences Education, Environment
    and Food Policy, Guyana

Jean-Louis André
Ministre, Ministère de l'Agriculture,
    des Resources Naturelles et du
    Development Rural, Haiti

John Junor
Minister of State, Ministry of
    Development, Planning and
    Production, Jamaica

Sergio Reyes
Subsecretario de Ecología, Secretaría
    de Desarrollo Urbano y Ecología,
    Mexico

Jaime Incer
Ministro-Director Instituto,
   Nicaragüense de Recursos
   Naturales y el Ambiente
   (IRENA), Nicaragua

Juan Alberto Manelia
Secretario Ejecutivo, Comisión
   Nacional del Medio Ambiente,
   Panama

Victor César Vidal
Subsecretario de Estado de Recursos
   Naturales y Medio Ambiente,
   Ministerio de Agricultura y
   Ganadería, Paraguay

Amaro Zavaleta
Jefe, Oficina Nacional de Evaluación
   de Recursos Naturales (ONERN),
   Instituto Nacional de
   Planificación, Peru

Naresh Singh
Executive Director, Caribbean
   Environmental Health Institute
   (CEHI) for the Ministry of
   Health, Labour, Information and
   Broadcasting, St. Lucia

Alpian Rudolph A. Otway
Parliamentary Secretary, Ministry of
   Health and Environment, St.
   Vincent and the Grenadines

Lincoln Myers
Minister, Ministry of Environment
   and National Service, Trinidad and
   Tobago

Raúl Lago
Ministro, Ministerio de Vivienda,
   Ordenamiento Territorial y Medio
   Ambiente, Uruguay

Enrique Colmenarea
Ministro, Ministerio del Ambiente y
   de los Recursos Naturales
   Renovables, Venezuela

Our Own Agenda (extracts)

LATIN AMERICAN AND CARIBBEAN COMMISSION
ON DEVELOPMENT AND ENVIRONMENT
INTER-AMERICAN DEVELOPMENT BANK
UNITED NATIONS DEVELOPMENT PROGRAMME

PROLOGUE

The Universe requires an eternity. . . . Thus they say that the conservation of this world is a perpetual creation and that the verbs, 'conserve' and 'create,' so much at odds here, are synonymous in heaven.
—Jorge Luis Borges, *Historia de la Eternidad*

Plight of a Small Planet: "Earth" Must Have No "Third World"

Environmental problems concern us all. No nations are peripheral. The search for environmental solutions must involve the North and the South and the East and the West. On "earth" there can be no "Third World".

The interrelated challenges of development and the environment require cooperation with the North. Only together can we find solutions to problems of international development (external debt, terms of trade and protectionism), threats to the environment (soil degradation, urban environmental problems, air and water pollution, loss of bio-diversity, climatic change, destruction of the ozone layer, and management of toxic wastes), the drug problem (production, consumption and trafficking), and the potential abuse of resources of the global commons (outer space and the Antarctic). Only together can we prevent human costs of even greater magnitude.

Solidarity and Complementarity

Cooperation between North and South is demanded partly because there exists an ecological complementarity between developed and developing countries. Developed countries are primarily located in the temperate regions of the world while practically all developing countries are located in the tropical ring. For the greater part the territories of developed countries offer better conditions for agriculture than those of the developing countries, many of which are covered by deserts, mountains, and tropical forests that limit agriculture.

Developed countries produce a food surplus while developing countries must import food. Developing countries are essential partners for global environmental security, especially for the restraint of greenhouse gases and the preservation of bio-diversity. Major technological progress in developing countries would enable them to produce all the food they will require in the future without being forced to reduce the global environmental security services that they are providing. This complementarity will require solidarity between North and South. It will entail the mobilization of financial and technological resources to reach common goals. It will demand the ability to renounce a confrontational style, to forsake a mindset of winners and losers, to forget old notions of separate worlds within this single planet.

Finding Peace

Humanity desires to consolidate peace. We are pleased with the relaxation of tensions between the superpowers and with the favorable environment that this brings to international co-operation. However, conventional, chemical and nuclear arms continue to be dire threats to humanity. We consider that the risk of nuclear war is still the single most important threat to the survival of humankind. While steps have been taken towards nuclear disarmament, the massive destructive capacity of the major powers remains intact. In addition to human suffering, armed conflicts still prevailing in some countries or regions cause major environmental impact on renewable natural resources and land degradation. The reduction of military expenditures is a common goal.

Past Financial and Ecological Debts:
A Maze that Must Be Straightened Out

The present economic crisis and environmental threats are rooted in defective patterns of development—the economy of opulence and waste in the North and the economy of poverty, inequity and pressing needs for short-term survival in the South. The challenge is to design a strategy of development in harmony with nature and with the needs of future generations. In developing countries, the link between poverty, population and environmental stress must be given increased attention.

In our region, increasingly, we see that poverty is both cause and effect of local environmental deterioration. This link between poverty and exploitation of natural resources helps reveal another linkage: the relationship between foreign debt and the region's environmental problems. The high interest payments on foreign debt between 1982 and 1989 led to a net transfer of capital from the region to the creditor countries of $200 billion. This has encouraged overexploitation of natural resources to meet pressing short-term needs and speedily increase exports. The 1980s have represented for the region a "lost decade". A substantial number of countries of the region have seen incomes reduced to levels reached one, two and even three decades ago. The regional GNP in 1988 was lower than that for 1978; the decline in the 1980s is also in sharp contrast with the previous decade's constant growth. In this context, recuperation of growth and development are a necessary condition to address pressing social and environmental issues. It is estimated that the region has an investment gap of $80 billion annually. This situation results in grossly inadequate financial investment in social infrastructure and detracts attention from urgent environmental concerns. Debt alleviation is essential for dealing with environmental problems.

The transfer of capital away from the region did not begin, of course, in the past decade. The industrial revolution was based in large part on the exploitation of non-renewable resources in the industrialized countries themselves, as well as in the developing countries, in a way which did not reflect their true cost in terms of conservation needs and environmental consequences. The progress of industrialized countries was thus based on deforestation and, in some cases, the predatory exploitation of natural resources. By thus exploiting nature, the industrialized countries have incurred an ecological debt with the world. This carries an obligation now to support development in order that it may not aggravate delicate conservation and environmental balances resulting from past neglect.

A common North-South agenda must include, first, the mobilization of financial resources on concessional terms to support environment and development action in the region and, second, a determination by the industrialized countries to develop and transfer environmentally sound technologies on a concessional basis. Latin America and the Caribbean are committed to the sustainable management of their ecological assets to help reverse the process of global environmental degradation and to preserve bio-diversity. However, the industrial countries must demonstrate an equal commitment to sharing the burden of the cost in a manner commensurate with their contribution to environmental degradation and their substantial ability to support and implement new environmental and development policies. The level of burden-sharing should reflect the accumulated environmental debt for which the industrial countries are primarily responsible, as well as the significant external financial support required to complement the internal efforts of countries in the region to eradicate critical poverty.

Developed countries should also facilitate access by the countries of the region to environmentally benign technologies on an affordable basis and to collaborate in joint research and development ventures aimed at accelerating production of new and existing technologies in our countries. This will have the added benefit of helping to transform and modernize the productive sectors of the economy.

Back in History: Lessons for the Future

Back in history, the people of Latin America and the Caribbean were motivated by a deep, almost religious relationship between man and his environment. There have been lapses over time; but these beginnings must serve as the foundation for the region's commitment to sustainable development. Preservation of indigenous cultural identity is important to the region's environmental and development perspectives. The Indian population of the region rightly demands to participate in the strategies planned for the development of the forest which it has been using, managing and preserving for centuries.

Our message is intended for our civilian society and for its leadership. We consider that strong political will and leadership are required to break the deeply rooted popular belief that land use has no social or ecological limits; that bodies of waters arc owned by individuals and are not available to benefit all society; that these resources can be exhausted or polluted with impunity; and that industry is not responsible for its wastes and emissions. Public education and participation are essential for environmental protection.

Our region has experienced a democratization process that should be sustained. The broad participation of civilian society is essential if we are to achieve development with equity. There currently exists a great movement for improving the quality of our democracy in ways that facilitate people-centered development while recognizing the legitimate role of the state, particularly in its enabling and regulatory function. These processes of governmental modernization and reform should be encouraged both for their wider purposes and the contribution they can make to achieving the goals of sustainable development.

We must develop legislation and institutions to address new emerging environmental problems and threats. Old structures must be modernized and local communities and authorities empowered and granted access to environmentally sound technologies, for they are closest to the needs and demands of their inhabitants. Non-governmental organizations, especially grassroots organizations engaged in harmonizing environmental needs and development, should be strengthened. The private sector must be encouraged to implement programs to arrest environmental degradation before it becomes irreversible. Participation of women in environmental protection, both in urban and rural areas, is essential to promote a positive behavior in youth and in the population in general. Major efforts shall be developed in the region to achieve these goals.

We consider it essential that new economic criteria and indicators be developed that take into account natural resources as stock of "capital." We must abandon policies which encourage over-exploitation of natural renewable resources; which promote the uncontrolled use of pesticides and herbicides; and which promote the inefficient use of energy. We must develop pricing and tax systems that provide incentives for environmental protection in industrial and other productive activities.

The Challenge for Building Sane Cities

Three out of four Latin Americans inhabit urban areas. An increasing number of urban inhabitants face inadequate basic services and housing and unsanitary conditions both at home and at work. The cities are plagued by severe problems of disorganized expansion, solid and liquid waste disposal and air pollution that make them vulnerable to natural disasters.

This process of urbanization with insufficient capital poses an impossible task for local authorities. Thus "informal cities" continue to grow at an accelerating rate around most Latin American metropolitan centers. For example, a city of 700,000 people is added each year to the periphery of Mexico City and one of 500,000 to the periphery of Sao Paulo. These cities lack the infrastructure or financial resources needed to cope with the current population or to absorb newcomers. Efforts must be made to disperse the population to medium-sized cities, but this in turn will depend on a dispersal of economic activity within a context of modern, decentralized government. The talent and creativity of the urban poor must be channelled into small community-based projects to provide housing and basic services.

Cities where industries are concentrated are often highly polluted and lack adequate social and sanitation infrastructure and proper policies for the treatment of hazardous industrial waste. Acid rain, commonly affecting industrialized countries, is increasing in industrial areas of Latin America and the Caribbean. Toxic wastes are being exported from industrialized countries and are causing major environmental problems. In several cases, industries not complying with environmental laws and regulations in the industrialized countries are being transferred to developing countries where these regulations are ignored.

The environmental challenges facing Latin America and the Caribbean concern human life and well-being. Exposure to hazardous waste presents unquestioned health risks. Seven of the 10 commonly found chemicals at waste disposal sites can cause cancer, seven can cause birth defects and five produce genetic damage. The combination of chemical residues, toxic wastes, car exhaust fumes and other consequences of uncontrolled urban pollution constitute major health threats to all, but particularly to children and the elderly.

Air pollution alone is a constant fact of life for 81 million urban residents of Latin America. The result is an estimated 2.3 million cases of chronic respiratory illness among children, 105,000 cases of chronic bronchitis among the elderly, and nearly 65 million days of work lost. The additional costs to already overburdened health care systems ultimately can be measured; pain and human misery cannot. Environmental pollution demands a concerted national and international response.

The Energy Dilemma

The region faces problems of insufficient energy use by large sectors of the population, emission of air pollutants, destruction of hydroelectric potential, deforestation due to over-utilization of fuel wood, over-exploitation of fossil fuels and inefficient transformation and use of energy.

The production, transformation, transport and utilization of various forms of energy generate positive and negative impacts. Adequate assessment of their environmental and social impacts, and particularly the potentially adverse consequences they entail for human health, should be undertaken. The region has vast hydropower reserves and renewable energy sources. Also, the potential for energy conservation is large. The region accounts for 20 percent of the world's hydroelectric potential; however, within the region, only one fifth of the consumed energy is produced by hydropower. While nuclear energy development in the region is limited, in some countries it may be necessary to utilize these sources in short or medium term. In these cases available environmentally-sound and secure technologies should be mobilized. For this, the support of developed countries is crucial.

Our Natural Heritage: A Fragile Potential

The ability to meet our continent's food requirements will suffer because of increasing land degradation and the resulting decline in agricultural productivity. The rural population remains at the mercy of the fragile characteristics of the natural resource base. Rural livelihood depends on climatic cycles which affect agricultural crop production. Farm output will also be harmed in the long term by the loss of genetic resources.

Modest increases in agricultural production in recent years were due largely to the excessive use of fertilizers and pesticides derived from fossil fuels. This trend creates the fear that the gradual exhaustion of petroleum sources will in coming years cause a decline in food production, especially in the poorer countries. These countries will be greatly affected since they are highly dependent on petroleum-based products and will also face greater demands for food as their population growth rates are high. Therefore, a consistent effort to improve productivity while conserving soil and water resources is vital for the region.

The region faces water management problems. Vast arid and semi-arid areas have limited water resources. Even in areas with abundant water resources, the distribution of these resources among countries and within countries varies widely. Clean water sources in some countries have been exhausted. Major hydrographic basins exhibit symptoms of degradation. The accumulation of large quantities of sediment in these basins causes frequent flooding, resulting in serious loss of life and property. Hydroelectric plants or irrigation systems should be constructed with adequate environmental safeguards. The situation in general calls for rational and efficient water management and use.

The region is endowed with vast biodiversity. Five out of the twelve richest countries in the world in terms of plant and animal species, the so-called "ecologically mega-diverse" countries, are in Latin America: Brazil, Colombia, Mexico, Peru and Ecuador. This vital biological reserve, which is of major importance both to the region and to the world, is being rapidly depleted. The continued loss of hundreds of tropical species, many without even being classified by science, is an issue of great concern for the region. The region should ensure that this heritage, which has medicinal, industrial and food potential, generate sustainable benefits for the local population. Reforestation, rehabilitation and recovery of degraded ecosystems should enjoy top priorities. Sustainable management of forests, involving other non-timber products, will promote social and economic objectives and the preservation of bio-diversity.

The Amazon: A Wealth to Sustain and Develop

The Amazon cannot be considered simply an ecological treasure and an important regulator of global climate; it is also a major develop-ment resource. The preservation of the tropical rain forests, and especially the Amazon forest, will depend on the mobilization of research and development, technology, and financial resources for sustainable management of this area. A commitment of support from the international community and voluntary co-operation of the eight sovereign Amazonian states is needed to preserve the Amazon as an asset for the region and for the world community.

To reach our goals, it is necessary to develop alternative technology adequate to maintain the fragile ecological equilibria of the region and simultaneously contribute to the countries' economic development. Ecological and economic zoning is a useful tool which should be expanded and promoted. The legal recognition of zoning and its close correlation with economic policies suited to the ecological reality of each zone are important elements for its success.

Preservation of the Amazon is of interest to the world community. However, it is of greatest interest to the Amazonian countries. The issue must therefore be debated by them on their own terms with the support of foreign scientists and an enlightened international public opinion. The issue at stake is the preservation of the forest and its bio-diversity, the control of atmospheric pollution and the development of the region. Agreements have already been formalized among sovereign countries of the Amazon basin. These constitute a starting point for more extensive actions.

Nature Unbounded: Thinking Like a River

Large and small river basins including the Amazon, the Orinoco and the La Plata River belong to several countries. Other shared ecosystems include the Andean Mountain System, the Amazon forest, the Caribbean Basin and the arid and semi-arid region shared jointly by Mexico and the USA. Management of these ecosystems requires common and joint action.

Rivers, seas and oceans know no boundaries. The main problems involving the use of marine resources are over-exploitation of some fish species, oil pollution and degradation of coastal resources and waterfront ecosystems, and the dumping of urban and industrial wastes and pollutants. The efficient and sustainable use of these resources would represent a major gain for the region. All coastal countries should develop coastal zone management strategies. This is especially important for countries in the Caribbean Basin and those threatened by rising seas and oil pollution, among others.

Only One Sky: We All Breathe the Same Air

With the end of the cold war, humanity must address other pressing issues such as the alleviation of poverty, development, equitable relations among nations and large-scale migrations caused by poverty and the environmental crisis. Global warming will have a major effect on the rise of ocean levels and is likely to cause other climate-related disasters which will also affect Latin America and the Caribbean.

If misguided energy policies are the principal causes of global warming and climate change, we must also point out the manner in which a disproportionate use of energy by some countries, particularly the industrialized nations, causes great harm to other countries and to the balance of the planetary system. Developing countries must participate effectively in international negotiations to protect the world's climate.

Depletion of the ozone layer will increase skin cancer and eye defects and will affect marine and terrestrial organisms. The contribution of Latin America and the Caribbean to the production of chlorofluorocarbons and halons is extremely small; 95 percent of these gases are produced by the developed world. Nevertheless, the consequences of the depletion of the ozone layer would be widely felt in the world. Industrialized countries must take measures to reverse this situation.

The production, demand, traffic and consumption of drugs is associated with health and environmental deterioration. Extensive productive lands in Latin America have been converted into cocaine plantations. Chemicals and pollutants used in cocaine cultivation and processing are dumped in rivers, spreading pollution. Co-responsibility of consumer and producer countries in this issue is essential.

The Antarctic possesses a unique ecosystem. The manner in which its rich resources should be exploited is extremely controversial. Its mineral and biological resources are desired by many nations. As a global commons, the Antarctic could provide scientific knowledge to many nations, especially in relation to climatic changes. The Antarctic Treaty is to be renegotiated in 1991. We consider it essential that the Antarctic be preserved for use in scientific research.

The use of outer space for communications and remote sensors possesses an economic value. The geo-synchronous orbit may be considered a finite global resource which is already creating conflict because of the large number of satellites in use. The future role of this resource must be defined to ensure that its benefits be equitably shared with developing countries.

Several countries in the region have suffered increasingly from natural disasters, particularly tropical storms (notably, in the Caribbean) and earthquakes (notably, in Central America). Disaster prevention and mitigation should become an integral part of development and environmental planning at local, national, regional and global levels. As evidence mounts of human responsibility for the intensification of such natural disasters, so does the responsibility for mitigating their consequences. There is need for such formalized sharing of the burden of natural disasters, particularly when the majority of the victims are among the world's poor.

We believe that these common endeavors must be carried out within an international and institutional framework—established at both the United Nations level and at the level of inter-American institutions. We should strive for global agreement on human actions to save our endangered habitat.

A Hundred Years of Non-Sustainability:
Reversing a History of Flawed Development

The call for sustainable development has been articulated by the World Commission on Environment and Development. Its report, Our Common Future, asserts that humanity has the capacity to make development sustainable—to ensure that it meets the needs of the present without compromising the ability of future generations to meet their own needs. This concept, noble and sound as it may be, must be made to work in economic and social terms. To do so, we must realize, first, that some of our resources have been substituted by others and, second, that we ourselves are using some resources too fast to serve either our long-term interests or the welfare of future generations.

Although our region retains a favorable ratio between resources and population compared with other regions of the world, we recognize the immense pressure on the capacity of the ecosystems to sustain the present population growth rate.

Because our region attaches high priority to meeting the needs of the almost 200 million people living in poverty, we must regain progress and development. Development should, however, be reoriented so that growth does not aggravate pollution and environmental problems. Economic growth must not become self-destructive.

Recent action by industrial countries to establish a modest fund to finance implementation in developing countries of the provisions of the Montreal Protocol on the Protection of the Ozone Layer is a step in the right direction. However, the implementation of large-scale and pervasive measures to redress current conditions requires that substantial additional concessional financing be channeled to the countries of the region in accordance with the specific priorities of those countries. In fact, a consensus among the countries of the region and of the industrial world that reflects mutually agreed and beneficial obligations is essential if we are to reverse global environmental degradation and ensure sustainable development in the near future. Various mechanisms have been identified for mobilizing the required financial resources for a Global Environmental Facility. These include among others: a "carbon-sink" levy, a CO_2 emission levy, a tax on oil levied on the users, and voluntary contributions by the industrial countries.

The quest for regional integration has been strengthened by growing global interdependency. Changing economic and political realities underscore the belief that strong nationalism represents a threat not only to global stability but also to the technological advances that have created a largely interdependent world, due in large measure to the speed of modern transportation and communications.

A Sense of Solidarity: A Future for Civilization

We are in the era of another major technological revolution. Its effects transcend national borders. The world is in a position to develop technologies that could render environmental degradation controllable. The industrialized nations must provide incentives for the development of environmentally sound technologies which prevent the production of harmful products and promote the efficient use of energy. A change towards a more environmentally conscious world requires that developing countries have easy and affordable access to such technologies.

Our continent must have a clear voice and strategy on environment and development issues. It is to help formulate this strategy that the United Nations Development Programme and the Inter-American Development Bank have sponsored the preparation of this report, in collaboration with ECLAC and UNEP. It draws on the thinking, analysis and debate that have taken place over the past decade in the region. A number of distinguished experts and scientists have directly contributed to the preparation of the report, and consultations have been carried out with diverse public and private sector groups. The report represents an attempt to draw upon these reflections, to provide a Latin American perspective on these issues—exploring new courses of action, rethinking the practices of flawed development that were followed in the recent past, and channeling political initiative and public participation into a development strategy which is not self-destructive.

"Our Own Agenda" seeks to contribute to development of a regional vision for the United Nations Conference on Development and Environment. Brazil 1992 must serve as a global forum in which efforts must be made to seek a balance between meeting the needs of today and providing for those of future generations. Our region places high priority on the discussion of those environmental issues clearly linked with development. At the heart of those issues is the urgent need to alleviate poverty and improve the quality of life of our people. It is in this way that Latin America and the Caribbean can construct a common future for the region and the rest of the world.

Mahatma Gandhi in his wisdom wrote, "How can we not be violent with nature when we are violent among ourselves?" Peace between our countries, peace within our countries in the framework of civil and pluralistic societies, peace with nature, harmonizing satisfaction of the basic necessities of today with those of tomorrow—these are the pillars of a new kind of development, a sustainable development in terms of politics, economics, philosophy, and ethics. Our Own Agenda must be one that acknowledges the eternity of the universe. Let us move forward together and call on all those who have the willingness to act generously and who are endowed with vision and a sense of solidarity for the present and future of human civilization.

—Latin American and Caribbean Commission on Development and Environment, August 27, 1990

INTRODUCTION

1.1 General Considerations

At the end of the decade of the 1980s it was evident that the world economy had undergone a prolonged period of sustained growth. At the same time, it was also evident that this growth was inequitable and was characterized by greatly increased poverty worldwide.

For the Third World, and particularly for Latin America, economic conditions have deteriorated seriously over the last 10 years. This is the combined result of growing external indebtedness, environmental deterioration over a number of years, the decline in the price of many basic export commodities, unfavorable trends in international commerce and the failure of the economic policies adopted by several countries to produce the desired results.

What impact does a "lost decade" have on a country's history? Is this simply a recurring cycle? Are we marking the start of a downturn, or is this a period of transition, an opportunity to change directions and take stock of ourselves? A country's development does not appear predetermined. Rather, it ebbs and flows in response to visionary mandates which are capable of projecting solutions and mobilizing the population in the face of challenges and the restrictions and opportunities presented by international conditions.

In the great uncertainty which presently faces Latin America and the Caribbean, there does not appear to have developed an awareness of the factors involved. As we approach the end of a millennium it is still not clear what the future holds for us. We should, therefore, begin to analyze the true nature and magnitude of the problems that affect us and the powerful forces that move in today's world. This obliges us to look at the large picture and examine the region's ills in an objective fashion.

The models of civilization that prevail in the world and that have produced important gains in human development for several decades have shown unmistakable signs of crisis. Signs of progress have been accompanied by worrisome evidence of environmental degradation and situations which lower the quality of daily life. In fact, the appearance of environmental problems threatens the ability to sustain this process of human development in the medium- and long-term.

Despite the achievement of enormous technological progress, large segments of the population still do not enjoy the benefits of economic growth; poverty is more intense and more widespread throughout the world. The more advanced countries increase their wealth exponentially and outpace the developing nations. In addition to the presence of grinding poverty, the latter are characterized by the emergence of social groups which have achieved high levels of income and consumption which are also proving to be unsustainable.

We are confronted, therefore, with a crisis situation basic to the civilization in which we live: the development model that we have adopted appears less viable with each passing day. Although changing this model might appear to present problems, continuation of the present model without modification is certain to prove even riskier. It does not appear feasible, therefore, for the Latin American and the Caribbean region to attempt to associate itself with a system which is viewed objectively as out-of-phase in the very countries in which it was judged a success in the past. It is essential, therefore, that these regional countries adopt different models of development which distribute the benefits of economic growth in a more equitable manner, which avoid a high level of environmental deterioration and which truly improve the quality of life—not only the per-capita income level—of present and future generations.

As in all crisis situations, ours presents opportunities for improvement as well as problems. To a degree, the crisis constitutes a denial of the validity of what has been done in recent years and the manner in which it has been done. For this reason, we may be less dependent on the past and more daring and creative in our future endeavors, thus preventing present and future problems. All of this is feasible if it is based on an objective evaluation of what constitute the great development problems of the region, the priorities that must be set for addressing them, and the manner in which they may be carried out successfully. Essential to this task is the development of strategies which contain methods and procedures by which we can achieve environmentally sustainable development.

It is crucial for Latin America and the Caribbean to begin to devise new action programs which will produce a genuine improvement in the quality of life of their populations. The strategies should signal ways and procedures which will enable us to avoid the stages and problems which those countries have had to follow which today enjoy the world's highest living standards.

The reordering of our flawed growth patterns will also require a dramatic change in the behavior of the industrialized countries and in the attitude and nature of their relations with us. Such are the economic and ecological consequences engendered by this behavior and so strong are the links of interdependence between those countries and our region that a radical modification of this relationship will be required if our efforts to correct the developmental methodology that we adopted in the past are to be successful.

To achieve these goals we must establish certain positions which will provide a solid basis for our undertaking. These must include agreement within the region as to what constitutes sustainable development; the causes of flawed development that led us to the current impasse; agreement on our environmental agenda; the strategical concepts underlying the type of development which we wish to achieve, and their global testing; our delayed involvement in the scientific-technological revolution now in progress, and the need to strengthen our capacity to negotiate with the North more favorable conditions for our sustainable development.

If we agree to a common regional position based on points such as those mentioned, it will be easier to set the goals which we ought to pursue. From the conversation which we are proposing there will develop points of agreement as well as disparities which must be settled in good time. A fruitful dialogue is essential if we are to reach agreements which will enable us to consolidate our positions and articulate methods and concepts. Because these concepts will be new, they must be explained to the national leadership and to the people of the region in order to develop awareness and gain support.

The preparation of a common strategy will enable us to enter into an effective dialogue with other Third World nations and with the North at the World Environment and Development Conference, to be held in 1992.

If we manage to chart our course and develop the collective will to achieve true development, the past will be little more than a unpleasant memory in the history of our peoples. To us falls the task of carrying out this plan.

1.2 The Need for Our Own Agenda

We must define our own environmental agenda. If we fail to evaluate objectively the problems and opportunities presented by the region's natural heritage, we cannot establish priorities for action and we will assuredly err in designing the strategies that we believe can provide us sustainable development. Environmental problems are always determined by the economic and social realities present in each development phase and by characteristics of the natural and social environment. It is up to us to point out those aspects which, because of their serious nature, require the most urgent attention.

The industrialized countries hesitate to link the environmental issue with underdevelopment. This is natural. The unsustainable patterns of consumption and dissipation of natural resources adopted by these countries have exerted an alarming impact on the environment. Throughout the decade of the 1970s development was considered the greatest cause of environmental degradation. But now in the 1980s we perceive that stagnation produces even worse effects. Economic crisis has produced a significant decline in per capita income in most of our countries; unemployment has increased while investments in health, education, housing and urban services have been reduced.

At the end of this decade, 200 million of our inhabitants lived in conditions of extreme poverty, and although it is inadmissible to attribute to the destitute the exclusive responsibility for contamination of their environment, we must accept the fact that poverty and environmental deterioration are parallel and interrelated effects of the same global process of flawed development[1]. As long as this mode of development persists, poverty will merely increase, further jeopardizing our future.

We must remedy many other situations as well. We refer to problems such as those derived from inadequate soil use and exploitation; deterioration of the environment in urban centers, which contain the bulk of our population; irrational exploitation of our most important ecosystems, the basis of our natural heritage; and permanent abuse of our water sources, to mention but a few.

These problems cannot be addressed, however, without taking into account such national and international economic factors as payment of an onerous service on the external debt and the decline in international commodity prices which, largely as a result of unemployment and poverty, force the region to abuse its natural resources.

1.3 The Need for a Special Strategy

There is no universal strategy for sustainable development. The most successful strategies are based on an analysis of our own regional institutional, economic and social peculiarities and of our environmental problems.

As we have pointed out, poverty is both the cause and the result of environmental degradation. Because it is the principal social problem which the region is called upon to solve, a basic strategy for achieving sustainable development must face up squarely to the problem of abject poverty. To correct this situation we must attack the very root of the problems which we wish to resolve as well as their consequences. In addition, we cannot treat the problems in a social-welfare manner, as we have in the past, but must attack the structural factors that underlie the phenomenon, among them the economic policies which contribute to impoverishment of the population and in large measure cause environmental degradation.

Amidst all of the problems affecting the fortunes of Latin America and the Caribbean, we have not been sufficiently discerning to note that these problems are closely linked with our concept of society and nature. We must change these attitudes if we are to devise a development strategy in harmony with nature. And, if this reforms and strengthens civil society and makes it more participatory, we will be establishing a mechanism for the creation of sustainable development. Men who are socially mobilized and have a deeply-felt need to solve their environmental problems will provide daring and creative corporate leadership in defense of their companies' environment and, simultaneously, of sustainable development.

The achievement of sustainable development also requires the establishment of a medium- and long-term planning mechanism. We have heard much talk, as though it were a purely theoretical matter, of the need to incorporate the environmental dimension into this planning. We begin to foresee that this will be possible on some type of territorial basis. If we are capable of exerting a deliberate effort to bring order to economic and social activities throughout the region, in harmony with environmental values, we will have taken two strong steps toward sustainable use of natural resources and control of contamination.

We would thus create conditions which would enable us to act preventively to control environmental degradation rather than simply to repair the damage, which is often irreversible, once it has been done. We will prepare to act upon the fundamental causes, which depend for the most part on the manner in which productive activities are carried out and on the population.

The achievement of sustainable development will require, among other things, the enactment of far-reaching reforms in order to modernize our governments. Weak structures characterized by inefficiency and corruption will not enable us to fill existing legal loopholes and even less guarantee the trial and punishment of those guilty of environmental crimes. Nor will we be able to rely on institutions capable of formulating and carrying out the medium- and long-term policies required by a sustainable development strategy.

1.4 The International Climate and Our Sustainable Development

The implementation of sustainable development in Latin America and the Caribbean will encounter obstacles whose origins are beyond its scope. Growing international interdependence, not always subject to the concepts of social justice, has produced asymmetries which obstruct its development. Many aspects of the matter must be discussed and resolved if we are to address this question in a truly adequate context. If not, we would invalidate all other strategies which we might formulate in this regard.

We must look with objective concern at the problem of industrial dispersal which is taking place in the more advanced countries as a consequence of the new technico-scientific revolution and stricter environmental safeguards which have gone into effect. This is giving rise to a process of relocation of industry to the south at the risk of reproducing environmental impacts which are now unacceptable to the industrialized world.

Another problem which is gaining in importance in the developing countries because of its grave and immediate consequences is the growing threat of becoming a kind of dumping ground for the industrialized countries. The danger implicit in this situation may reach a dimension similar to that of the drug traffic, with all the corruption and environmental destruction that such entails.

Beside problems with direct environmental connotations, to which we have referred in part, other problems of an economic nature include:

- The outflow of capital from Latin America and the Caribbean to the developed countries
- The constant deterioration of the prices of the raw materials produced by countries of the region
- The fluctuation of interest rates, fundamental in the worsening external debt problem (see Figure 1)
- The introduction of inappropriate technological patterns, and
- Commercial protectionism, among others

It is imperative that all these problems be discussed at the start of the international dialogue on ways to achieve worldwide sustainable development. Clearly this concept would not be feasible if it were presented on the understanding that it would be applicable only within national bounds.

1.5 The Need to Strengthen Our Negotiating Capacity

The agenda items that we propose for discussion form part of the concerns that we share with the rest of the developing countries, and with whom we make up three quarters of the world population.

One must understand that, whatever effort is made to link development and the environment, important economic costs are involved which the developed nations are in a relatively better position to pay. The agenda can be

Figure 1 Latin American and the Caribbean: Net Capital Income and Net
Transfer of Resources (Billions of Dollars)

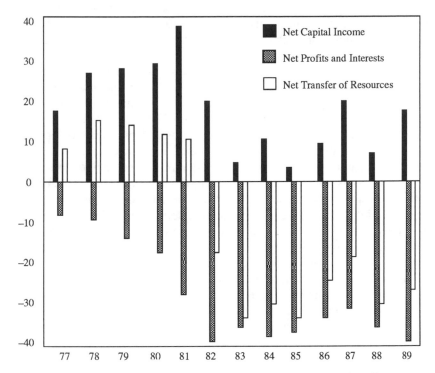

Source: ECLAC. *Preliminary Balance of the Latin American and Caribbean Economy.*
December 1989. Graph 10.

implemented, therefore, only if agreement is reached to designate
responsibilities in accordance with the financial capacity of each country.
Together with the need to institute programs to conserve the world's great
ecosystems, Latin America and the Caribbean face an important challenge in
preserving the productivity of their own ecosystems.

The negotiations must also discuss priority items in order to provide a
context favorable to sustainable development. Without the prospect of
an enduring peace which will enable countries to dismantle their
conventional, nuclear and chemical weapons, we will continue to live under
the threat of an irreversible environmental cataclysm. However, the relaxation
of tensions among the great powers, evidence of which we are now
witnessing, will permit the channeling of important resources now being

spent on armaments into the implementation of sustained development on a worldwide basis.

For its part, discussion of the drug problem as an agenda item is of great relevance. There is no contaminant with such destructive potential for society as drug addiction, especially when it is centered in the youth and in the intellectual and management sectors.

When we sit down with the North to discuss a common development and environment agenda, we must be aware of those factors that make us weak and those that contribute to the strength of our positions. We know that at the present time we constitute an impoverished and indebted region, susceptible of being pressured by the countries of the North which because of the crisis have strengthened their positions. For that reason, we must remember that as well as accumulated liabilities the region possesses invaluable assets, including an abundance of natural resources which may form the basis of a sustainable development for all mankind, as well as the potential of its rich biodiversity and cultural heritage, valuable resources in their own right. Those assets, furthermore, are enlarged by the substantial environmental debt that the industrialized countries have run up with the region over time and which has not yet been paid.

Here we have the fundamental ideas which have guided the analysis and evaluation of the situation and the formulation and selection of strategies and action plans outlined in the following section of this document. They are the points on which there has been considerable consensus and conviction that it is necessary to destroy myths and to establish, with an element of modesty, viable solutions for our society.

·   ·   ·   ·

A NEW INTERNATIONAL PACT
FOR SUSTAINABLE DEVELOPMENT

One of the most singular contributions and, given its universal nature, perhaps the most transcendent message of the report from the World Commission on Environment and Development was the statement that the future of nations, both industrial and less developed, is tied to an inexorably common destiny, not in the form of parallel tracks in the same direction, but interconnected in multiple ways that have made the world an interwoven skein that can lead all of us down unpredictable paths.

Interdependence is one of the present-day phenomena that have greatest impact on the fate of nations. The balances of political power; cultural events transmitted instantly by telecommunications; technological progress, which has contributed so much to homogenization of the civilization model; social phenomena, such as poverty, extending to the farthest corners of the world;

and ecological impact that crosses borders to take on planetary magnitude—all are links in this inescapable concatenation.

5.1 Under the Sign of Interdependence

If the multiple bonds that characterize interdependence are convincingly present in any field, it is in the field encompassing development and the environment. Human civilization is moving toward a global state. This is apparent in all dimensions: social, economic, cultural, and political, as well as environmental. But the transition is not occurring smoothly and harmoniously: it is turbulent and beset with conflict.[2]

At present, sustainable development cannot possibly be conceived as an autarchic process, but is inextricably situated—in any country or region—in the international context. All the more so when we recognize the uneven geographic distribution of natural resources and the technologies to explore them, which are the basis of economic management, thus requiring ongoing negotiations for their use. Let us not forget that most of the natural resource base currently being utilized in this planet is located in the Third World; and that it has been subjected to continuous and intense degradation, largely due to the development policies and exploitation systems created by the industrial countries and imposed by them for so many years.

The sharp hikes in international oil prices in the early 70s blessed the producer countries with vast trade surpluses. A significant percentage was deposited in international banks, where it joined the mounting tide of dollars stemming from the United States' trade shortfall. The banks, for their part, adopted an aggressive policy of loans at floating interest rates, most of which went to governments and private companies in countries of the region and to the Third World in general.

The situation began to change radically in the second half of the decade. World economy and trade began to sag, and the immense public deficit incurred by the United States began to be financed by a dramatic increase in flows of foreign funds, attracted by rising interest rates that soared to four times historic levels.

The availability of money for new loans to developing countries dried up abruptly, and the debtors' ability to pay declined due to the worsening terms of trade, interest rates far above the traditional rates on the basis of which the external debt had been contracted, and poor management by many countries of the resources obtained through that indebtedness.

In the 1980s, the world economy was dominated first by a pronounced recession, followed by recovery on the part of the industrial countries, high real interest rates, declining real prices for basic commodities, worsening terms of trade, and the plummeting of voluntary private financing to many developing countries. The economic and technological gap between the industrial countries and those of the region continued to widen.

When the governments of Latin America and the Caribbean adopted austerity policies to pay their external debt, the poor were the first to suffer the consequences due to the sharp cuts in many programs and public services, food subsidies, health care, housing, and the like. As a result, the trend to regressive distribution of income increased at the expense of the poorest population sectors. The external debt crisis and the consequent adjustment measures triggered a 14 percent downturn in the region's real per capita income between 1980 and 1986. Numerous wage earners, who until then had belonged to the middle class, dropped below the poverty line. The wages of the poorest workers also declined in most cases, even more sharply than average income. Urban unemployment fell from 6.9 to 11.1 percent, and the number of underemployed rose, while social expenditures underwent appreciable cutbacks in 14 of the 19 countries for which information is available. All of these factors show that the recession was accompanied by intensified inequities and poverty. The enormous effort expended to service external debt has obviously added an alarming amount to the social debt. At the same time, net transfers from the region to the developed countries between 1982 and 1987 are estimated at US$145 billion, equivalent to about one-third of their domestic savings. Despite all these dire figures, the debt has not diminished but continued to mount, rising from US$285 billion dollars in 1981 to US$415.9 billion by year-end 1989—i.e., five times the total value of the region's exports.[3,4]

Global economic changes, coupled with powerful international processes, have thus reinforced each other, drastically altering the region's prospects for economic growth and reducing much of its endogenous decision-making capacity. Those global changes are generating grave local effects.

The need to obtain foreign exchange from exports to pay the interest on the debt and import the inputs essential to production creates new pressures to increase agricultural output—even in unsuitable areas—and in certain cases to overexploit the natural resources, resulting in low prices for raw materials that do not cover the cost of production and, in the case of tropical wood, to manage natural timberlands.

Between 1976–80 and 1981–85, the rate of deforestation in tropical areas rose by 3.6 percent. The direct causes, on the one hand, are the activities of entrepreneurs who took advantage of tax policies favoring the lumbering trade, an increase in largescale stockraising, and speculation in land, all of which were also motivated by government-backed development projects. On the other hand, the opening of new access roads, expulsion of poor peasants to marginal areas, and demographic growth—which is usually stimulated by poverty—resulted in exacerbated pressure on the ecosystems of tropical woodlands in various countries.

Given the fragility of some ecosystems in the face of activities that take no account of their ecological characteristics, the most frequent result has been impoverishment and destruction of the soil's productive capacity: a problem that affects the living conditions of hundreds of millions of persons. But the problem does not end there. The enormous biomass accumulated in the exuberant vegetation of tropical rain forests is frequently burned uselessly to introduce an ephemeral and unsustainable agriculture which contributes to global climatic deterioration.[5]

The worsened economic situation of countries in the region makes it very difficult to adopt measures for environmental conservation and sustainable use of natural resources and has a particularly sharp effect on cutbacks in budgetary allocations for investment in environmental programs. Although the economic crisis has eroded the number of new development ventures, thereby reducing the environmental impact associated with large-scale infrastructure works and agricultural development, it will necessarily increase the pressures on deforestation by needy peasants and the new marginal sectors. Aside from the effects that are already visible, the increasing social impoverishment and reduction in development expenditures bode ill for the region's social, economic and environmental future. The circle has closed. Global economic changes have conspired to create conditions that foster deforestation of the region through multiple local activities in a context of mounting social pressures and reduced options. Local poverty then contributes to degradation of the global environment, whose regulation capacity has already been saturated, mainly by the activities of the industrial countries, which in turn will affect the economies and living conditions for all the inhabitants of the planet, rich and poor, sparking social tensions.[6]

5.2 Agenda for Negotiations with the North

Given the convincing nature of these factors, the path to follow is obvious. As we noted earlier, everything in the world scenario is tightly interrelated— the problems that affect us as well as their solutions. It is thus impossible to conceive of a strategy for sustainable development of Latin America and the Caribbean that is isolated from its context, and most particularly from events in the industrial countries. The world's problems today are so huge that they can only be resolved with a joint or global approach, not by spot treatment, no matter how powerful a country may appear to be.[7]

Since our strategy is conceived as a process of profound change in different orders, we must realize that this process will be viable only to the extent that there is an equally important change within the developed countries themselves, and in the factors underlying their international relation with us.

It is particularly important to establish a fruitful dialogue, conducive to a new solidarity pact that will put us all on the path of sustainable development. This is not a question of the application of international social justice standards alone, but a response to a common instinct for survival. Achievement of this aim, however, will require the adoption of new approaches to problems affecting both North and South. It will be necessary to inspire an ethic that allows the common interests of nations to prevail over those of individuals; that affords a more objective appreciation of the great risks faced by humankind unless we resolve situations which, like the rampant poverty or changes in climate, compromise global stability; that starts with the premise that progress is not viable in the long term if it is not conceived as a process enabling all countries—not just a group thereof—to realize their development aspirations in an equitable and egalitarian manner, and lets us address the problems that affect us from the vantage point of the longer term.

In order to couch the discussion in practical terms, we in the region must reach a consensus on an agenda of the principal problems to be negotiated with the North. The list must necessarily include items of the following nature, but this does not mean that consideration cannot be given to other crucial matters that may arise.

A. Peace and World Disarmament

Without peace there can be no sustained development, in the region or in the world. The principal threat to peace was created and is maintained by the great powers, particularly by their nuclear arsenal that despite notable progress in East-West relations continues intact and in a way is strengthened by such initiatives as the so-called "Star Wars." Our region considers it immoral and therefore unacceptable for the great powers to overlook the fact that the greatest and most absolute threat to the environment will not be discussed in the context of North-South relations.

For our part, we should commit ourselves to live in peace, to eliminate regional geopolitical tensions and, consequently, to lower our military expenditures. Ideally, such outlays should be limited to the need to guarantee internal security.

B. A New Economic Relationship

Without economic growth, there will be no development, much less sustainable development. Latin American and Caribbean economic growth has ground to a halt, mainly due to the burden of enormous external debt.

Accordingly, the industrial countries cannot brush this topic or the restoration of financial flows for the region aside if they really support the aim of making sustained development the mainstay of a more just and happy world. Both parties should not delay tackling the search for innovative alternatives to resolve this key problem equitably.

C. Facing Poverty

Although favorable resolution of the previous point is indispensable for coming to grips with impoverishment in the long term, we must acknowledge the existence of other global mechanisms that are also generating poverty and need to be revised. The so-called structural adjustment policies, for example, are a case in point. In many instances they heighten the dimensions of the social crisis created by the application of adjustment measures adopted by governments to be able to meet external debt service payments; the unilateral reduction of the prices of raw materials produced by developing countries, and the export of capital-intensive and labor-saving technologies to those countries.

Our countries should also undertake the commitment to implement the reforms needed to effect a more equitable distribution of income so that we may attack poverty at its roots. This will give us moral force when it comes to negotiating, since it will show that we have the will to correct conduct that has proved undesirable in the past.

D. Economic Policies Constraining
Sustainable Development of the Region

In the developed countries one finds economic policies whose effect is completely contrary to that of the sustainable development strategies that may be employed by our region. This is the case, for example, with trade policy. "So long as the North promotes the liberalization of regional markets, its trade policies are discriminatory and frequently interfere with market forces when this is in their interests."[8] Other policies, such as those embodying farm subsidies, technological development in respect to intellectual property rights, exporting of toxic wastes and contaminant technologies, and industrial deployment based on relocation and export of commodities that are prohibited in the North, warrant substantive revision in conjunction with the negotiations.

E. Utilization of Natural Resources

A variety of factors involved in the management and consumption of natural resources should be discussed. They include:

- The prices of raw materials that include external items and the cost of regenerating natural resources that have been exported
- International treaties and agreements on the use of information contained in biodiversity
- Conditions for use of our genetic potential in biotechnologies developed in industrial countries
- Conditions for importing technologies adaptable to our ecosystems
- The costs entailed by international requirements for management of our natural resources

F. The Treatment of Global Environmental Problems

No topic requires handling by multilateral negotiating mechanisms more than this one, since we have seen that our responsibility for generating global environmental problems is much smaller than that of the developed countries. It is proposed that consideration be given to such points as:

- Contributions to, and conditions for, solving the greenhouse effect in terms of control of the destruction and burning of biomass and forest plantings that serve as carbon sinks, among other topics
- The implications and costs of complying with the Basel Agreement on Transborder Transport of Highly Toxic Wastes, the Protocol of Montreal, and other agreements currently undergoing negotiation

G. New Mechanisms to Finance Execution of Environmental Conservation Programs

This is a focal point for activating a regional environmental conservation policy that posits action in proportion to the size of existing problems. The resources available in existing multilateral financial assistance organizations are completely inadequate for this purpose, so it behooves us to explore the constitution of new instruments—for example, international funds that mobilize resources to be used for that purpose. Consideration has been given, in this connection, to establishing fees for the use of nonrenewable natural resources, specifically the consumption of fuels of fossil origin. Various mechanisms have been identified for mobilizing the required financial resources for a Global Environment Facility. These include among others: a "Carbon-sink" levy, CO_2 emission levy, tax and oil levies on the users, and voluntary contributions by the industrial countries.

In this context, debt-swap operations provide a meaningful opportunity. Some of the numerous debt-swap options are more expedient than others for specific countries and cases, and they should therefore be carefully scrutinized.

H. Scope of Technical Cooperation

Because of the vast opportunities in this field which they offer both the recipients of the cooperation and those providing it, consideration must be given to programs and new channels for the transfer of knowledge and technologies, conceived in accordance with the region's sustainable development priorities, and taking precautions to make sure that they are suitable for our ecosystems and sociocultural conditions. There are a number of fields which are urgently in need of this type of program. Examples are:

- Support for the development of university education, particularly the formation of middle management and workers specializing in natural resources and environment
- The use of new technologies to conduct studies to determine the potential of specific ecosystems and techniques for prudent management thereof
- Research in leading-edge technologies, such as biotechnology
- Establishment of environmental information systems for land use planning purposes and the possibility of interconnecting such systems to set up a regional network

I. Conditionalities with Respect to Environment

The developed countries—directly through their representatives in financial organizations and indirectly through nongovernmental organizations—are imposing severe environmental conditionalities on investment in Latin America and the Caribbean. We are not opposed to the general concept that new investments should be environmentally sound. On the contrary, our countries' environmental legislation also endorses those precautions. But we oppose arbitrary use of environmental criteria to create insurmountable barriers to development, particularly when those criteria are supported by private agendas backed by press exaggerations and an uninformed public opinion. Along the same lines, it behooves us to investigate ways to evaluate projects in terms of their impact on sustainable development, for simple extrapolation of the North's criterion to the South is unrealistic and counterproductive.

J. Financial Cooperation Required to Implement the Sustainable Development Strategy

The implementation of sustainable development strategies for Latin America and the Caribbean will require financing that is beyond the capacity of the region's domestic savings. IDB and ECLAC estimates indicate that the region has an investment deficit of some 80 billion dollars a year, due in part to the debt and the worsened terms of trade.

There is an inescapable need, therefore, to create financial cooperation programs which could be supported by a large international environmental fund.

This fund, in turn, could be administered by the multilateral development agencies, among them the World Bank and the Inter-American Development Bank, as well as by such multilateral technical cooperation agencies as the United Nations Development Programme. The fund should address itself in a highly concessional fashion to a variety of investment projects and not just those relating to the environment, as is presently the case with the so-called Global Environment Fund. Although important and meritorious in its own right, the GEF would stop giving priority to the more urgent problems of Latin America, such as urban environmental, water and soil problems, which are the basis of nutritional safety.

K. Change in Consumption Patterns in the North

The industrial countries' heavy consumption of natural resources is a threat, not only to sustainable development in global terms but also to the natural heritage of the Third World, which is the prime supplier of those commodities. The bargaining tables will therefore have to address this topic objectively, for the success of those negotiations in rationalizing that situation will have direct and positive consequences for us.

L. Handling of the Drug Issue

A global strategy to eliminate drugs requires real North-South cooperation in every stage, including demand, trafficking, and production. It will entail a cutback in consumption in the North and alternative development for the peasants in the South.

M. Population

We recognize the enormous obstacle our still-excessive population growth places on regional development. Quite some time ago, our politicians and intellectuals stopped defending the thesis of population growth as a positive growth factor, as is evident in the declining demographic indicators. On the other hand, neither can we accept the family planning policies frequently proposed by the developed countries and which are not in tune with our reality. No matter how difficult it may be, a cutback in population growth can be achieved only by dint of the minimum economic growth indispensable for improving education and the quality of life, raising them to levels compatible with human dignity.

5.3 Towards a New International Agreement

Within the countries themselves the responsibility for implementing sustained development rests jointly with all leadership groups. All will benefit alike, or together suffer the consequences of underdevelopment.

The same situation applies at the global level. Each country must share in this mission, whether it does so alone or in conjunction with others. We have observed how interdependence makes us all links in a process that leads us to a common destiny.

The programs needed to create a viable and equitable future for mankind must not rest on simple rhetoric, lest we run the risk of remaining mired in our present predicament. This will require a commitment to cooperation rather than "aid" and to solidarity and the common good rather than confrontation and the gratification of personal desires.[9]

Whether the outcome will improve or worsen our condition will depend on our ability to find ways to work together productively—within a framework of mutual help, each in accordance with the means at his disposal. Only this can justify the Pact that we are proposing from the point of view of international social justice.

This commitment to work together in harmony with nature is based not only on moral principles but also on political, economic and ecological imperatives which can be weighed objectively and which are perhaps even more decisive.

Winds of liberty and democracy are sweeping the globe. This makes it imperative that we tackle the problem of poverty in the Third World. "As we approach the third millennium, we must fashion a global security concept which incorporates the notion of sustainable development, the need to face up to underdevelopment, the inequitable distribution of wealth, the degradation of the environment and the depletion of our resources."[10]

In the economic sphere, we can point out that the lack of balance that exists between the industrialized countries cannot be resolved exclusively within northern borders. The United States, for example, can balance its budget and improve its balance of payments only with the simultaneous economic growth of the surplus countries. Otherwise, it will reduce world demand and precipitate a drop in production and world trade. Any adjustment by the North during a period of world economic growth and high employment must inevitably involve the South in a solution. Therefore, economic adjustment in the North and the debt crisis in the South are closely interconnected.[11]

As for ecology, it has been clearly shown how the model of civilization developed after the industrial revolution has generated an environmental crisis on a worldwide scale, the solution of which involves us all under the threat of inciting a universal cataclysm.

An international agreement to achieve sustainable development on a world and regional scale would not only relieve tensions which have already become unbearable but would help usher in a new era of global prosperity which would permit mankind to reach higher levels of well-being without those asymmetries that offend the spirit.

In addition to establishing new agreements between the North and the South, such a pact should enable us to strengthen relations between ourselves. Never has the need to move ahead on regional integration been as clear, particularly in light of the challenges now facing us. We are so badly separated—and there is so much to be gained by a closer union—that we must make a major effort to establish agreements towards this end. We must reach agreement among ourselves first before we undertake negotiations with the North. This will strengthen our hand and will reinforce the mutual conviction that we are working toward a far-reaching goal, namely that of building a better future for our peoples.

Such a pact, furthermore, opens wider the road to peace; it will be of inestimable value in this respect. The danger of global, regional or local conflict is lessened not only by the reduction of nuclear and conventional weapons but by the elimination of the causes of tensions that could become unbearable. One of the principal advantages of the program that we are proposing is that it makes possible a development model which is more equitable in its relations with the environment and in its contribution to the world at large.

5.4 Some Instrumental Considerations

The launching of such a laudable undertaking will also require the adoption of precautionary measures to overcome obstacles and avoid misunderstandings.

First, the document must be subjected to an exhaustive analysis in political, scientific and cultural fora in Latin America and the Caribbean as well as in the developed countries in order to create a consensus, which will be indispensable, and to round out the theme.

This debate could culminate in the meeting of the Presidents and Chiefs of Government of the Latin American and Caribbean nations to adopt a sustainable development strategy for the region, preparatory to a World Environmental and Development Conference to be held in Brazil in June of 1992.

Once we have established a regional position, as soon as possible we should open negotiations with the developed countries leading to the signing of an International Pact which commits us to work jointly for sustainable development. It is to be hoped that this process may culminate on the occasion of the United Nations Environment and Development Conference to be held in Brazil in 1992. This will permit us to demonstrate the tangible results that can be achieved through the application of regional approaches derived from well-thought-out and consensual positions devoid of any trace of prejudice.

It will be the responsibility of the United Nations organizations, including the UNDP and the World Bank, as well as the IDB and other multilateral assistance agencies and all public and non-governmental institutions that chose to support this plan, to stimulate within their special spheres of activity a discussion of the programs contained therein. This will round out and adapt the programs to the unique characteristics and requirements of the countries of the region where they will be applied.

One of the main aspects of this overall undertaking will be the Environmental Action Plan in Latin America and the Caribbean which, under the stewardship of the UNDP and within the parameters outlined in this document, is now being developed. This action plan is designed primarily to strengthen and direct joint regional and international efforts to face up to priority environmental problems at the subregional, regional and global levels.

Another important aspect of these deliberations is to achieve greater coordination in the use of the international funding earmarked for sustainable development projects in the region. Although these resources are clearly insufficient at present to handle existing needs, it is essential that we establish new regional programming mechanisms which will enable us to put these resources to more effective use. It is essential, therefore, that we reach a consensus as to our true priorities, and that is one of the objectives of this document.

Sustainable development requires an international institutional framework. The United Nations system and the inter-American system as represented by the Organization of American States are called to play a central role. It is within the jurisdiction of these systems that our countries will participate in a discussion of policies, in the establishment of priorities, and in the equitable assignment of resources. Both systems should be strengthened and renovated.

FINAL OBSERVATIONS

We have no time to waste. Certain situations are becoming untenable and it is therefore imperative to enter into agreements to attempt to resolve them. We are talking about the generally deteriorated quality of life in the region. In addition to the oft-cited increase in poverty, there are: the dwindling size of the middle class; the decline of health care; lack of individual security, aggravated by socioeconomic conditions; the number of school dropouts; the impossibility of purchasing goods and services that were formerly obtainable; the many indications of an accelerated downward spiral of a worsening quality of life that is daily perceptible; the irremediable burden of grief that situation places on the majority of our population; and—perhaps even more serious—the collective loss of hope.

We are becoming a community of skeptics. We had thought that, however belatedly, we were nearing the state of sustained growth. But we see that we have lost a great deal of ground we had managed to cover, by dint of heroic effort, over a long period of years.

A visit to the developed countries will convince anyone from the region who has the slightest power of observation that the gap which separated us is deepening, particularly in the fields of scientific and technological development.

Most of our countries have traditionally had a national project. The establishment of democratic and constitutional governments has been the common aim of such undertakings. Our national histories are characterized by an unflagging struggle to attain that objective. We have suffered under authoritarianism for many decades. Peoples living in other latitudes had almost begun to believe that there was no fertile soil for freedom in Latin America and the Caribbean. Now, however, we have finally managed to stabilize democracy as a system of government. This augurs better prospects, if we can only preserve and perfect the institutions we have worked so hard to build. Unfortunately, however, the social tensions now being generated can lead to new setbacks. The loss of democracy would put an end to our long-cherished dream of a civilized way of life.

These sensitive circumstances are compounded by another factor, which also compromises our future irremediably: the destruction, often irreversible, of our natural heritage, nonrenewable resources which we exploit unceasingly, without foreseeing the damage their early depletion will wreak—accelerated degradation of our ecosystems, the basis of all present and future economic activity. Our shabby treatment of nature presages even greater social poverty. In addition, such action on our part also compromises the future of the other nations of this planet, which will also have to suffer the consequences of our ecological crisis.

In light of this triple threat, the most sensible course of action is to establish the basis for a *Pact with the North*. Its foundations will be solid to the extent that we are able to work in tandem. Let us go forward together and call on all those who are in a position to act generously and who are endowed with vision and a solidary sense of survival to join us at the bargaining table.

NOTES

1. United Nations Environment Programme (UNEP), "Medio ambiente y desarrollo en América Latina y el Caribe: Una visión evolutiva." Documento preliminar para discusión. Mexico, D. F. Part IV. pp. 24.

2. Gallopin, G. C. 1990. Ambiente y desarrollo.

3. Higgins, G. M., H. H. Kassam, L. Naiken, G. Fisher and M. M. Shah. "Potential population supporting capacities of lands in the developing world." Technical Report Project "Land resources for population of the future." FAO/FNUAP/IIASA. Rome. 1982.

4. ECLAC. Balance preliminar de la economía de America Latina y el Caribe. December, 1989.

5. Gallopin, G. C. 1990. Ambiente y desarrollo.

6. Gallopin, G. C. 1990. Ibid.

7. Ferrer, A. A New International Solidarity. Photocopied. Buenos Aires. December, 1988. pp. 1.

8. Ferrer, A. 1988. Ibid., p. 3.

9. Gallopin, G. C. 1990. Ambiente y desarrollo, p. 18.

10. Brudtiand, G. Address to the 44th session of the United Nations General Assembly. September 25, 1989.

11. Ferrer, A. 1988. A New International Solidarity, p. 2.

Central American Agreement for the Protection of the Environment

W E, THE PRESIDENTS OF THE REPUBLICS of Costa Rica, El Salvador, Guatemala, Honduras and Nicaragua, aware of the need to establish regional cooperation mechanisms for the rational use of natural resources, the control of pollution, and the reestablishment of ecological equilibrium;

CONVINCED that, to improve the quality of life of the Central American peoples, it is necessary to promote respect for the environment in the setting of a model of sustainable development so as to avoid the injurious effects of earlier models on the natural resources in the region;

AWARE that, in view of the intimate interdependence among the countries of the isthmus, regional cooperation must be a primary instrument for the solution of ecological problems;

AND CONFIDENT that regionwide regulation of the use of natural resources and the environment is a fundamental factor for the attainment of a lasting peace;

Have decided to sign the present Agreement, which shall be named the

AGREEMENT ESTABLISHING THE CENTRAL AMERICAN
COMMISSION FOR THE ENVIRONMENT AND DEVELOPMENT

Chapter I, Article I: ESTABLISHMENT. Under the present Agreement the Contracting States establish a regional regime of cooperation for the optimal and rational use of the natural resources in the area, the control of pollution, and the reestablishment of ecological equilibrium in order to improve the quality of life of the population of the Central American isthmus.

Article II: PURPOSES. The present regime is established for the following purposes:

a. To develop and safeguard the high diversity of the biota and ecosystems and of the Region's natural patrimony;
b. To establish collaboration among the Central American countries in the search for and adoption of sustainable styles of development, with the participation of all parties concerned with development;
c. To promote coordinated action by governmental, nongovernmental and international entities for the optimal and rational use of the natural resources in the area, the control of pollution, and the reestablishment of ecological equilibrium;
d. To seek the regional and international financing needed to accomplish the purposes of the present regime;
e. To strengthen the national agencies charged with the management of natural resources and the environment;

f. To support harmonization of the broad lines of national policy and legislation with the strategies for sustainable development in the region, and, in particular, to incorporate the environmental considerations and parameters into the national development planning processes;

g. To determine the priority areas of action, including environmental education and training, the protection of shared watersheds and ecosystems, the management of tropical forests, pollution control in urban centers, the importation and management of toxic and hazardous materials, and other aspects of environmental degradation that impair the health of the population and the quality of its life;

h. To promote participative, democratic and decentralized environmental management in the countries of the region.

Chapter II. Institutional Provisions, Article III: The Central American Commission for the Environment and Development is created and consists of representatives named by the governments of the several countries. Each government shall designate one principal delegate to the Commission.

The Commission shall be assisted in its functions by the following entities:

a. the Chair of the Commission;

b. the Secretariat; and

c. such ad hoc technical committees as the Commission may establish for the performance of its functions.

Article IV: The Commission shall direct and administer the regime referred to in the present Agreement.

Article V: FUNCTIONS AND FACULTIES OF THE COMMISSION. The Commission shall:

a. Frame strategies for promoting environmentally sustainable development in the countries of the area;

b. Draw up a plan of action for the implementation of those strategies;

c. Approve its own Rules of Procedure and the requisite financial and administrative regulations;

d. Direct the work of the Secretariat and oversee the administration of the Fund established by the Agreement;

e. Designate its own Chairman, who shall be its Legal Representative.

Article VI: THE CHAIR. The Chairman shall act as the Commission's Representative vis-à-vis third parties, and shall convoke and chair its meetings. He shall be authorized to delegate functions to the Secretary as he sees fit. The office of Chairman shall be held for a term of one year, and shall be rotated among the member countries in alphabetical order.

Article VII: THE SECRETARIAT is the executive organ of the Commission, and gives effect to the resolutions assigned to it by the Commission and its Chairman.

Article VIII: THE SECRETARIAT has the following functions:

a. To carry out the decisions of the Commission, and especially to implement the Plan of Action it establishes;
b. To provide technical advice to the Commission in matters of its competence and to frame proposals for how best to accomplish the purposes of this Agreement;
c. To coordinate and direct the technical committees that the Commission shall establish;
d. To coordinate technical cooperation between the member countries and multilateral organizations;
e. To administer the Fund provided for in the Agreement in accordance with the regulations laid down by the Commission;
f. To administer the personnel of the Secretariat in accordance with such regulations as the Commission shall issue;
g. To represent the Commission in such matters as the Commission shall entrust to it;
h. To coordinate operations in each country with its principal delegate or with such national technical representation as he shall designate.

Article IX: THE TECHNICAL COMMITTEES shall advise the Commission and perform specific tasks as assigned by it. They shall be coordinated by the Secretary.

Chapter III, Article X: The Commission shall promote the allocation of human, material and financial resources to the programs and projects it sponsors. To this end it shall approach and negotiate, at its discretion, with the governments of the Contracting Parties, other governments and international organizations, regional and world development agencies, and national and international entities of any kind.

Article XI: The Commission shall have for the performance of its functions its own net worth, consisting in a fund to be constituted with:

a. Contributions to be made by the Contracting States.
b. The income in grants and other contributions that the Commission may receive.
c. The property that the Commission may acquire in any way.
d. Any income earned by the Commission's own property and financial resources.

Chapter IV. General Provisions, Article XII: The Commission shall ensure that the benefits in the form of material, human and financial resources generated by the application of this Agreement are apportioned equitably to all the countries parties to it.

Article XIII: RATIFICATION. This Agreement shall be submitted to the signatory States for ratification in accordance with the domestic legislation of each country.

Article XIV: DEPOSIT. The instruments of ratification shall be deposited in the Ministry of Foreign Affairs of the Republic of Guatemala.

Article XV: EFFECTIVE DATE. This Agreement shall enter into force, for the first three ratifying countries, eight days after the date on which the third instrument of ratification is deposited, and for the remaining countries on the date of deposit of their respective instruments of ratification.

Article XVI: AREA OF APPLICATION OF THE AGREEMENT. The programs and projects referred to in the present Agreement may encompass geographic areas that are of importance for the protection of the ecosystems in the area.

Article XVII: SETTLEMENT OF DIFFERENCES. Any differences arising on the application or interpretation of this Agreement shall be resolved, at the request of any of them, first by negotiation by a commission to be appointed by the States themselves. If said commission is unable to resolve the differences, recourse shall be had to the mechanisms established in international law for the settlement of differences.

Article XVIII: DURATION. The Agreement shall remain in effect for ten years counting from its effective date, and shall be renewed for successive periods of ten years. The present Agreement may be denounced by any signatory State. The denunciation shall take effect for the denouncing State six months after it has been deposited, and the Agreement shall continue in force among the other signatory States so long as at least three of them remain parties to it.

It witness whereof, we, the Presidents of the Central American Nations, have affixed our signatures to the present Agreement in the city of San José, Costa Rica, on the twelfth day of December, nineteen hundred eighty-nine.

Oscar Arias
President of Costa Rica

Vinicio Cerezo
President of Guatemala

José Azcona
President of Honduras

Daniel Ortega
President of Nicaragua

Alfredo Cristiani
President of El Salvador

The Tlateloco Platform

PLENARY SESSIONS AT MINISTERIAL LEVEL
Conference Room Document
MIN/5/Rev. 1
March 7, 1991

Meeting in Mexico City, March 4–7, 1991, the ministers and representatives of the Latin American and Caribbean member states of the Economic Commission for Latin America and the Caribbean (ECLAC), participants in the Regional Preparatory Meeting of the United Nations Conference on Environment and Development hereby:

1. *Reaffirm* the scope of resolution 44/228 of the United Nations General Assembly on environment and development in the search for a just and equitable new international order, as well as that of resolutions 45/211 and 45/212; also reaffirm the *Brasilia Declaration*, the *Action Call* of the Seventh Ministerial Meeting, and request the developed countries and international agencies to lend their firm support to the *Action Plan for the Environment of Latin America and the Caribbean*. They are pleased to endorse the document entitled *El desarrollo sustentable: transformación productiva, equidad y medio ambiente*, prepared by ECLAC, and the report of the Commission on Development and Environment of Latin America and the Caribbean entitled *Nuestra propia agenda.*

2. *Express* their deep concern that in the 20 years since the Stockholm Declaration was approved there has been severe deterioration in the status of the environment and serious degradation of global ecosystems. Such degradation is closely linked to the unsustainable models of development prevalent above all in the developed countries.

3. *Note* the significant achievements made in the region in the consolidation of democratic processes, peace-keeping, and respect for human rights.

4. *Recognize* that, despite the enormous efforts made to resolve the economic crisis, the underlying causes of the economic and social problems of the region still persist, including the external debt problem, thus triggering an alarming setback in the level of wellbeing of the majority of the population, an increase in the number of inhabitants who live below the poverty threshold, and deterioration in environmental quality. Without a just and lasting solution to the external debt problem, the Latin American and Caribbean states cannot attain sustained and environmentally sustainable economic and social development.

4(bis). *Further recognize* the vulnerability of small island states to the vicissitudes of the global environmental and economic climate.

5. *Stress* that the sustainability of development necessary in order to reverse that degradation will entail an effort involving the entire international community. Fundamental support for that effort must come from the most developed regions possessing the most resources, based on their greater responsibility in the global process of environmental degradation.

6. *Note* the contribution, in that global effort, that the region can make to the protection and improvement of the environment, given its resource potential, and express their commitment to prevent continuing degradation for the sake of present and future generations.

7. *Recognize* the need to strengthen horizontal technical cooperation, to support the adoption of regional agreements, and to have the region participate more fully in the solution of global and regional environmental problems.

8. *Further note* that the environmental dimension is an integral part of the development process and therefore cannot be considered separately. In addition to the internal effort, a favorable international economic setting is essential in order for such development to be environmentally sustainable.

9. *Maintain* that the promotion of sustainable development is incompatible with the introduction of new forms of environmental and economic conditionality or with restricted access to technology. The international commitment to protecting and improving the environment demands that access to environmentally sound technologies not be based on purely commercial terms. Furthermore, the higher costs entailed in the transfer of environmentally sound technology should be assumed by the developed states.

9(bis). *Affirm* that environmental issues should not be used as a pretext for unjustifiable barriers to international trade.

10. *Affirm* that international, regional and subregional instruments for the solution of environmental problems of a global nature ought to include rules for the effective transfer of technology, institutional arrangements for better ways and means to integrate the environmental dimension into development, specific mechanisms for lending and financing on concessional terms in such a way that the developing countries can honor their commitments.

11. *Affirm* their conviction that the United Nations Conference on Environment and Development represents a unique opportunity for significant decisions to be reached that would ensure the transfer of environmentally sound technologies and the flow of new and additional financial resources, to the end that the developing countries may duly include the environmental dimension in their development plans and objectives.

12. *Express* the need to stimulate science and technology research and

development for the purpose of enhancing regional and national technology management capabilities for sustainable development. Global and sectoral research projects ought to be undertaken, aimed at clearly identifying the roadblocks to development and access to such technologies. In those same areas institutional and organizational conditions should be improved, as well as science and technology information systems. A special international fund should be set up to ensure the developing countries access to and transfers of environmentally sound technologies and to reinforce their own endogenous capability.

13. *Consider* it essential to develop human resource training capabilities with emphasis on pertinent specialties related to the management of the natural resources of the region in terms of potential, use and maintenance.

14. *Emphasize* that the solution of environmental problems and the promotion of sustainable development at the national level largely depend on international cooperation, including financing. In this respect, a special fund should be created with a view to providing the developing countries with new and additional concessional resources so as to allow them to carry out environmentally sound development programs and projects in accordance with their national development objectives, priorities and plans. Contributions to that fund should not be siphoned off from current allocations to international cooperation in the sphere of economic development. The eligibility criteria for funding for the implementation of such programs and projects should not be based solely on the criterion of per capita income currently applied by the multilateral lending institutions.

15. *Resolve* that the current patterns of production, distribution and consumption prevalent mainly in the developed economies should be redesigned so that our countries may raise their living standards and quality of life and reconcile gains in productive efficiency with the principles of environmental improvement and social equity.

16. *Emphasize* that the common struggle against poverty, particularly extreme poverty, entails far-reaching changes in social and economic policies. Efforts to link environmental improvement and development should recognize local and global responsibilities and take into account the close interrelationship between poverty and environmental deterioration. Those efforts will be successful to the extent that they are the result, among other factors, of access to acceptable living standards, adequate levels of social organization, political representation and real participation by the people in the definition of their own development.

17. *Recognize* that sound management of the natural heritage is an essential prerequisite to economic growth and sustainable development. Retrospective and prospective methods should be studied that would allow the value of the natural heritage and its depreciation to be assessed.

18. *Coincide* in the need to supplement national facilities for environmental regulation and control existing in the region today with broader economic and financial measures, policies and incentives that would include in the decisions of all sectors the social and environmental costs of the activities of each one of them, and meet the economic, social and environmental goals of development.

19. *Recognize* that, given the vital need for an active commitment by all sectors of society to promote environmental protection and improvement and sustainable development, the coordinated participation of nongovernmental organizations and of other sectors of society should be encouraged in the preparation of and during the Conference, as well as in the implementation of its mandates.

20. *Point out* that current development patterns have ignored the importance of cultures living on the fringes of such development. In order to attain sustainable development the importance of those cultures must be fully recognized, given their cumulative and extensive knowledge and understanding of the natural world and the means they have developed for its use and sustainable management.

21. *Affirm* that the United Nations Conference on Environment and Development, throughout its preparatory process as well as in the related international negotiations, particularly those aimed at finding a solution to global environmental problems, ought to ensure the observance of the following tenets, among others: principle 21 of the 1972 Stockholm Declaration concerning respect for the sovereignty of States over their natural resources and all their economic activities; the integration of the environmental dimension as an inherent element of the process of equitable and sustainable development; the interdependence of global and local problems, particularly social, economic and environmental problems; rejection of economic and environmental conditionality; equitable sharing of responsibility, and the precautionary principle.

22. *Declare* that, bearing in mind decision 1/25 of the Preparatory Committee for the United Nations Conference on Environment and Development, in addition to the issues mentioned earlier, the following environmental topics are of major importance to the Latin American and Caribbean region, and should therefore be dealt with by the Preparatory Committee as well as by the Conference in Brazil.

a) Protection of the Atmosphere and Climatic Change

Latin America and the Caribbean, in participating in the solution of the global environmental problems affecting the atmosphere, do so taking into consideration their own limited responsibility in the generation of such environmental problems. Involvement in any solution agreed upon should be consistent with the technical and economic resources available to the developing countries.

The negotiation of a frame convention on climatic change with a view to its adoption by UNCED and based on the best scientific evidence available, should seek to minimize the anthropogenic causes of climatic change and its possible adverse effects. Whereas the latter could well be far-reaching, the archipelagos, islands and countries with low-lying coastal areas in Latin America and the Caribbean will be among the most vulnerable areas.

In that joint effort, consideration should be given to the respective importance of the sources and concentrations of greenhouse gases, and the attendant obligations under the convention be expressed in accordance with the contribution of both aspects to the problem or to its solution.

The convention should be consistent with the primary responsibility of the developed countries for the concentrations and net emissions of greenhouse gases in the atmosphere and the effects of transboundary pollution. Likewise, the need of the developing countries to capitalize on their natural resources in an environmentally sustainable manner should be recognized, to the end of raising the living standards and quality of life of their people in an environmentally sustainable fashion.

Under the Vienna Convention and the Montreal Protocol and its amendments, the region should work towards the primary goal of the replacement of substances that deplete the ozone layer, and in that sense should have all the technical and financial assistance needed to implement programs in the science and technology area, short of undertaking new external borrowings.

b) Biodiversity and Biotechnology

The Latin American and Caribbean region attaches great importance to the conservation and sustainable management of its ecosystems in order to preserve their biological diversity, which is a fundamental, sovereign part of the national heritage of States that possess such diversity.

A nation's knowledge of its own biodiversity at both the scientific and grassroots levels is part of its scientific and cultural heritage; therefore, any cross-border utilization should be duly regulated and controlled by the country of origin. The region should encourage in international forums the institution of legal instruments for the protection of the genetic heritage, its population structure and ecosystems, as well as adequate regulation of trade deriving therefrom.

Advances in biotechnology and the economic potential for exploiting biodiversity require that there be an international agreement for setting up transparent mechanisms, subject to the express consent of the proprietary State of the original genetic resources, to govern such areas as controlled access, commercial development or their use for scientific purposes. Those mechanisms should also include specific provisions for sharing on an equitable footing the benefits of such development or use. Furthermore, the developing countries should have access to state-of-the art biotechnology on concessional terms and to information on the biological and ecological safety of technologies developed earlier.

A convention on the conservation of biological diversity ought to include commitments for its conservation as well as benefits and obligations relating to biotechnology.

c) Protection and Management of Terrestrial Resources

The problems here should be focused from the standpoint of comprehensive environmental planning and management both prospectively and in the long term, consistent with the principles of eminent domain and environment-development as a comprehensive approach.

Planning in terms of specific resources, areas or activities should be targeted to and in keeping with the thrust of national environmental land-management planning and economic planning in order to move in the direction of harmonious spatial use.

The problems of deforestation, desertification and drought require taking comprehensive measures to reverse those processes and guarantee the conservation and management of ecosystems, while at the same time respecting the sovereignty of States over their own natural resources.

Forests: The economic and ecological potential of the austral, temperate, tropical and boreal forestry ecosystems should be the centerpiece of discussions for reaching agreement on multilateral measures for the protection of natural ecosystems and support for their sustainable management by States having such ecosystems.

Such measures—not necessarily mandatory—should be complementary to international instruments on forest/climate and forest/biodiversity interrelationships, on which specific legal instruments are being negotiated.

The measures should consider: economic assessment of forestry resources, the needs of population groups dependent on such resources, and strategies for the orderly use, protection and reclamation of those ecosystems, including the involvement of local communities. With that objective in mind, ways and means of international cooperation to support such activities ought to be established, including financial and technology-transfer mechanisms.

Forestry management should be a priority goal among actions to prevent deforestation that should be taken into account in the negotiations and in arranging financing for the use and conservation of the forest ecosystem. Harvestable and non-harvestable products entering the marketplace should come from forests managed sustainably in accordance with each country's own criteria.

d) Soil Degradation (acidification, erosion and salinization)

The acute process of soil degradation, to a greater or lesser extent, affects every country in Latin America and the Caribbean. Degradation is the consequence of improper rural and crop development styles, based mainly on overworking the land in order to maximize short-term income or, from the standpoint of rural peasants, in order to survive. The degradation processes are clearly encouraged by the predominantly applied technologies, whether in farm systems that foster intensive use of the land or in the drive to expand the crop and livestock frontier. A greater support effort for developing countries in order to prevent and combat soil degradation should be an international priority, carried out through technical cooperation, technology transfers and support for the generation of autochthonous and environmentally sound technologies, scientific research, manpower training, and financing.

e) Protection and Management of Oceans, Seas and Coastal Areas

The region typically has wide diversity in terms of marine, coastal and ocean resources, which may be capitalized on for the benefit of the population of the region. Deterioration of the marine and coastal resources as a result of chaotic exploitation and pollution originating in the sea or on land poses a serious problem for coastal and riverine countries that depend on those resources in order to meet socio-economic and development goals. Consequently, the regional oceanic program in the wider Caribbean and southeast Pacific, as well as other regional cooperation programs, such as the South Atlantic one, should be strengthened, including the legal instruments of earlier agreements.

The benefits derived from the use of the resources for development must be optimized, while at the same time abuse of those resources must be minimized. This requires:

• Conducting an inventory of living and non-living resources in order to assess their potential and possible extraction indices.
• Setting aside "special areas" based on the nature of the resources, their dynamics, sensitivity, and such uses as may be made of them, as well as their degree of interdependence.
• Conducting regional and international sharing of data from national stations systematically monitoring changes in coastal dynamics.

• Developing appropriate technologies among developed and developing countries relating to such spheres as aquaculture, desalinization, sea-bed mining and others, including implementation of the precautionary principle and the clean technology approach.

• Expanding the inter-connections and relationships among regional and subregional agencies and programs and developing the scientific, technical and financial capability to carry out research, follow-up, information exchanges and technical assistance for the proper management of marine and coastal resources.

• Supporting the establishment of regional marine technology centers for joint development of environmentally compatible technologies leading to sustainable development of the region.

• Encouraging integrated management approaches to marine and coastal areas and their resources.

• Banning the dumping of toxic wastes in seas and oceans, and designing ways and means to protect those resources against exploitation by third-party States.

• Urging the international community to create ways and means of cooperation for the conservation and optimal use of marine resources within the area of sovereignty or jurisdiction of two or more riverine States or on the high seas.

• Promoting the need for a worldwide agreement to safeguard the marine environment from pollution of terrestrial origin, bearing especially in mind the responsibility assigned to the regional economic commissions under Resolution A/44/228 of the General Assembly, *inter alia*.

f) Protection of Fresh Water Quality and Supplies

The need to protect fresh water quality and supplies is vital to the region. Therefore, it is essential to take measures aimed at safeguarding and conserving water resources and development sites. The following proposals are made with that purpose in mind:

• The financing and implementation of watershed management plans in a manner conducive to the orderly development of natural resources and better conditions for human settlements in those areas.

• The establishment of regional strategies and programs for the comprehensive development and conservation of water resources that would guarantee balance in economic growth, environmental protection and national and international watershed management as a guarantee of sustainable development.

• Identification of water resource supplies and potential and assessment of the environmental repercussions of their use.

• Establishment of the research and oversight programs needed to reduce or do away with fresh water pollution.

g) Eradication of Poverty in Human Settlements

Coping with critical poverty and its linkage with environmental degradation at the national level will require a rebound in the growth rate, structural reforms, and a change in economic and social policies. A priority matter would be to provide prompt and adequate health and education services, plus better housing and related services in rural and urban areas.

In addition to the endogenous effort to eradicate poverty, arrangements must also be made for international cooperation in the interrelated areas of trade, external debt, the additionality of financial resources and technology transfers.

h) Urban Development and Environment

The cities of Latin America and the Caribbean, generally speaking, are inadequately funded, thus leading to insufficient basic services, high rates of marginality and deterioration of the urban environment. Financing mechanisms for sustainable development based on spatial planning should lead to higher living standards and a better quality of life in urban and rural settlements.

Along these lines, the new financing mechanisms for sustainable development should attach due priority to this problem in the areas of housing, sanitary conditions (potable water supplies and sewer systems), solid and liquid waste disposal and air pollutions.

Environmental Waste Management, Especially Toxic and Hazardous Wastes

The regional agreements complementary to the Basel Convention should be given preferential attention with respect to the mechanisms for follow-up and prevention of illicit traffic in toxic and hazardous wastes and dangerous products, which poses a potential threat to the environment of the region and to developing countries in general.

Successfully dealing with this problem will require the prompt adoption of a protocol to the Basel Convention setting up appropriate procedures on accountability and indemnity for damage emanating from transboundary movements and handling of hazardous wastes.

Whereas the developed countries continue to export harmful or hazardous substances, products, processes and technologies to the developing countries which are banned in the countries of origin, a mechanism should be established to prohibit their marketing.

23. *Repeat* their intent to continue their efforts and to achieve positive, concrete results in the negotiations conducted in the Preparatory Committee and ask the Secretary General of the Conference to bear in mind the proposals contained in this declaration in preparing the Conference documentation.

24. The participants express their gratitude to the people and Government of Mexico for their warm hospitality and for the full facilities provided for the meeting, which contributed to its success.

Stockholm Declaration on the Human Environment

The United Nations Conference on the Human Environment, having met at Stockholm from 5 to 16 June 1972, and having considered the need for a common outlook and for common principles and standards, adopted a DECLARATION ON THE HUMAN ENVIRONMENT to inspire and guide the peoples of the world in the preservation and enhancement of the human environment. Many of the 26 principles of the Declaration have since been included in other international declarations and resolutions and have become part of national policies in a number of the Member States of the United Nations.

THE DECLARATION PROCLAIMS THAT

1. Man is both creature and molder of his environment, which gives him physical sustenance and affords him the opportunity for intellectual, moral, social and spiritual growth. In the long and tortuous evolution of the human race on this planet a stage has been reached when, through the rapid acceleration of science and technology, man has acquired the power to transform his environment in countless ways and on an unprecedented scale. Both aspects of man's environment, the natural and the man-made, are essential to his well-being and to the enjoyment of basic human rights—even the right to life itself.

2. The protection and improvement of the human environment is a major issue which affects the well-being of peoples and economic development throughout the world; it is the urgent desire of the peoples of the whole world and the duty of all Governments.

3. Man has constantly to sum up experience and go on discovering, inventing, creating and advancing. In our time, man's capability to transform his surroundings, if used wisely, can bring to all peoples the benefits of development and the opportunity to enhance the quality of life. Wrongly or heedlessly applied, the same power can do incalculable harm to human beings and the human environment. We see around us growing evidence of man-made harm in many regions of the earth: dangerous levels of pollution in water, air, earth and living beings; major and undesirable disturbances to the ecological balance of the biosphere; destruction and depletion of irreplaceable resources; and gross deficiencies harmful to the physical, mental and social health of man, in the man-made environment, particularly in the living and working environment.

4. In the developing countries most of the environmental problems are caused by underdevelopment. Millions continue to live far below the minimum levels required for a decent human existence, deprived of adequate food and clothing, shelter and education, health and sanitation. Therefore, the

developing countries must direct their efforts to development, bearing in mind their priorities and the need to safeguard and improve the environment. For the same purpose, the industrialized countries should make efforts to reduce the gap between themselves and the developing countries. In the industrialized countries, environmental problems are generally related to industrialization and technological development.

5. The natural growth of population continuously presents problems on the preservation of the environment, and adequate policies and measures should be adopted, as appropriate, to face these problems. Of all things in the world, people are the most precious. It is the people that propel social progress, create social wealth, develop science and technology and, through their hard work, continuously transform the human environment. Along with social progress and the advance of production, science and technology, the capability of man to improve the environment increases with each passing day.

6. A point has been reached in history when we must shape our actions throughout the world with a more prudent care for their environmental consequences. Through ignorance or indifference we can do massive and irreversible harm to the earthly environment on which our life and well-being depend. Conversely, through fuller knowledge and wiser action, we can achieve for ourselves and our posterity a better life in an environment more in keeping with human needs and hopes. There are broad vistas for the enhancement of environmental quality and the creation of a good life. What is needed is an enthusiastic but calm state of mind and intense but orderly work. For the purpose of attaining freedom in the world of nature, man must use knowledge to build, in collaboration with nature, a better environment. To defend and improve the human environment for present and future generations has become an imperative goal for mankind—a goal to be pursued together with, and in harmony with, the established and fundamental goals of peace and of world-wide economic and social development.

7. To achieve this environmental goal will demand the acceptance of responsibility by citizens and communities and by enterprises and institutions at every level, all sharing equitably in common efforts. Individuals in all walks of life as well as organizations in many fields, by their values and the sum of their actions, will shape the world environment of the future. Local and national governments will bear the greatest burden for large-scale environmental policy and action within their jurisdictions. International co-operation is also needed in order to raise resources to support the developing countries in carrying out their responsibilities in this field. A growing class of environmental problems, because they are regional or global in extent or because they affect the common international realm, will require extensive co-operation among nations and action by international organizations in the common interest. The Conference calls upon

Governments and peoples to exert common efforts for the preservation and improvement of the human environment, for the benefit of all the people and for their posterity.

Principle 1: Man has the fundamental right to freedom, equality and adequate conditions of life, in an environment of a quality that permits a life of dignity and well-being, and he bears a solemn responsibility to protect and improve the environment for present and future generations. In this respect, policies promoting or perpetuating *apartheid*, racial segregation, discrimination, colonial and other forms of oppression and foreign domination stand condemned and must be eliminated.

Principle 2: The natural resources of the earth including the air, water, land, flora and fauna, and especially representative samples of natural ecosystems, must be safeguarded for the benefit of present and future generations through careful planning or management, as appropriate.

Principle 3: The capacity of the earth to produce vital renewable resources must be maintained and, wherever practicable, restored or improved.

Principle 4: Man has a special responsibility to safeguard and wisely manage the heritage of wildlife and its habitat which are now gravely imperilled by a combination of adverse factors. Nature conservation including wildlife must therefore receive importance in planning for economic development.

Principle 5: The non-renewable resources of the earth must be employed in such a way as to guard against the danger of their future exhaustion and to ensure that benefits from such employment are shared by all mankind.

Principle 6: The discharge of toxic substances or of other substances and the release of heat, in such quantities or concentrations as to exceed the capacity of the environment to render them harmless, must be halted in order to ensure that serious or irreversible damage is not inflicted upon ecosystems. The just struggle of the peoples of all countries against pollution should be supported.

Principle 7: States shall take all possible steps to prevent pollution of the seas by substances that are liable to create hazards to human health, to harm living resources and marine life, to damage amenities or to interfere with other legitimate uses of the sea.

Principle 8: Economic and social development is essential for ensuring a favourable living and working environment for man and for creating conditions on earth that are necessary for the improvement of the quality of life.

Principle 9: Environmental deficiencies generated by the conditions of underdevelopment and natural disasters pose grave problems and can best be remedied by accelerated development through the transfer of substantial quantities of financial and technological assistance as a supplement to the domestic effort of the developing countries and such timely assistance as may be required.

Principle 10: For the developing countries, stability of prices and adequate earnings for primary commodities and raw material are essential to environmental management since economic factors as well as ecological processes must be taken into account.

Principle 11: The environmental policies of all States should enhance and not adversely affect the present or future development potential of developing countries, nor should they hamper the attainment of better living conditions for all, and appropriate steps should be taken by States and international organizations with a view to reaching agreement on meeting the possible national and international economic consequences resulting from the application of environmental measures.

Principle 12: Resources should be made available to preserve and improve the environment, taking into account the circumstances and particular requirements of developing countries and any costs which may emanate from their incorporating environmental safeguards into their development planning and the need for making available to them, upon their request, additional international technical and financial assistance for this purpose.

Principle 13: In order to achieve a more rational management of resources and thus to improve the environment, States should adopt an integrated and co-ordinated approach to their development planning so as to ensure that development is compatible with the need to protect and improve the human environment for the benefit of their population.

Principle 14: Rational planning constitutes an essential tool for reconciling any conflict between the needs of development and the need to protect and improve the environment.

Principle 15: Planning must be applied to human settlements and urbanization with a view to avoiding adverse effects on the environment and obtaining maximum social, economic and environmental benefits for all. In this respect projects which are designed for colonialist and racist domination must be abandoned.

Principle 16: Demographic policies, which are without prejudice to basic human rights and which are deemed appropriate by Governments concerned, should be applied in those regions where the rate of population growth or excessive population concentrations are likely to have adverse effects on the environment or development, or where low population density may prevent improvement of the human environment and impede development.

Principle 17: Appropriate national institutions must be entrusted with the task of planning, managing or controlling the environmental resources of States with the view to enhancing environmental quality.

Principle 18: Science and technology, as part of their contribution to economic and social development, must be applied to the identification, avoidance and control of environmental risks and the solution of environmental problems and for the common good of mankind.

Principle 19: Education in environmental matters, for the younger generation as well as adults, giving due consideration to the underprivileged, is essential in order to broaden the basis for an enlightened opinion and responsible conduct by individuals, enterprises and communities in protecting and improving the environment in its full human dimension. It is also essential that mass media of communications avoid contributing to the deterioration of the environment, but, on the contrary, disseminate information of an educational nature, on the need to protect and improve the environment in order to enable man to develop in every respect.

Principle 20: Scientific research and development in the context of environmental problems, both national and multinational, must be promoted in all countries, especially the developing countries. In this connection, the free flow of up-to-date scientific information and transfer of experience must be supported and assisted, to facilitate the solution of environmental problems; environmental technologies should be made available to developing countries on terms which would encourage their wide dissemination without constituting an economic burden on the developing countries.

Principle 21: States have, in accordance with the Charter of the United Nations and the principles of international law, the sovereign right to exploit their own resources pursuant to their own environmental policies, and the responsibility to ensure that activities within their jurisdiction or control do not cause damage to the environment of other States or of areas beyond the limits of national jurisdiction.

Principle 22: States shall co-operate to develop further the international law regarding liability and compensation for the victims of pollution and other environmental damage caused by activities within the jurisdiction or control of such States to areas beyond their jurisdiction.

Principle 23: Without prejudice to such criteria as may be agreed upon by the international community, or to standards which will have to be determined nationally, it will be essential in all cases to consider the systems of values prevailing in each country, and the extent of the applicability of standards which are valid for the most advanced countries but which may be inappropriate and of unwarranted social cost for the developing countries.

Principle 24: International matters concerning the protection and improvement of the environment should be handled in a cooperative spirit by all countries, big or small, on an equal footing. Cooperation through multilateral or bilateral arrangements or other appropriate means is essential to effectively control, prevent, reduce and eliminate adverse environmental effects resulting from activities conducted in all spheres, in such a way that due account is taken of sovereignty and interests of all States.

Principle 25: States shall ensure that international organizations play a co-ordinated, efficient and dynamic role for the protection and improvement of the environment.

Principle 26: Man and his environment must be spared the effects of nuclear weapons and all other means of mass destruction. States must strive to reach prompt agreement, in the relevant international organs, on the elimination and complete destruction of such weapons.

UN General Assembly Resolution on the Conference on Environment and Development

RESOLUTIONS ADOPTED ON
THE REPORTS OF THE SECOND COMMITTEE

44/228. UNITED NATIONS CONFERENCE ON ENVIRONMENT AND DEVELOPMENT
Date: 22 December 1989   Meeting: 85
Adopted without a vote   Report: A/44/746/Add.7

The General Assembly

Recalling its resolution 43/196 of 20 December 1988 on a United Nations conference on environment and development,

Taking note of decision 15/3 of 25 May 1989 of the Governing Council of the United Nations Environment Programme[161] on a United Nations conference on environment and development,

Taking note also of Economic and Social Council resolution 1989/87 of 26 July 1989 on the convening of a United Nations conference on environment and development,

Taking note of Economic and Social Council resolution 1989/101 of 27 July 1989 entitled "Strengthening international co-operation on environment: provisions of additional financial resources to developing countries",

Recalling also General Assembly resolution 42/186 of 11 December 1987 on the Environmental Perspective to the Year 2000 and Beyond and resolution 42/187 of 11 December 1987 on the report of the World Commission on Environment and Development,[162]

Taking note of the report of the Secretary-General on the question of the convening of a United Nations conference on environment and development,[163]

Mindful of the views expressed by Governments in the plenary debate held at its forty-fourth session on the convening of a United Nations conference on environment and development,

Recalling the Declaration of the United Nations Conference on the Human Environment,[164]

---

161. See *Official Records of the General Assembly, Forty-fourth Session, Supplement No. 25* (A/44/25), annex 1.
162. A/42/427.
163. A/44/256-E/1989/66 and Corr.1 and Add.1 and 2.
164. See *Report of the United Nations Conference on the Human Environment* (United Nations publication, Sales No. E.73.11.A.14 and corrigendum).

Deeply concerned by the continuing deterioration of the state of the environment and the serious degradation of the global life-support systems, as well as by trends that, if allowed to continue, could disrupt the global ecological balance, jeopardize the life-sustaining qualities of the Earth and lead to an ecological catastrophe, and recognizing that decisive, urgent and global action is vital to protecting the ecological balance of the Earth,

Recognizing the importance for all countries of the protection and enhancement of the environment,

Recognizing also that the global character of environmental problems, including climate change, depletion of the ozone layer, transboundary air and water pollution, the contamination of the oceans and seas and degradation of land resources, including drought and desertification requires actions at all levels, including the global, regional and national levels and involving the commitment and participation of all countries,

Gravely concerned that the major cause of the continuing deterioration of the global environment is the unsustainable pattern of production and consumption, particularly in industrialized countries,

Stressing that poverty and environmental degradation are closely interrelated and that environmental protection in developing countries must, in this context, be viewed as an integral part of the development process and cannot be considered in isolation from it,

Recognizing that measures to be undertaken at the international level for the protection and enhancement of the environment must take fully into account the current imbalances in global patterns of production and consumption,

Affirming that the responsibility for containing, reducing and eliminating global environmental damage must be borne by the countries causing such damage, must be in relation to the damage caused and must be in accordance with their respective capabilities and responsibilities,

Recognizing the environmental impact of material remnants of war and the need for further international co-operation for their removal,

Stressing the importance for all countries to take effective measures for the protection, restoration and enhancement of the environment in accordance, *inter alia*, with their respective capabilities, while at the same time acknowledging the efforts being made in all countries in this regard, including international co-operation between developed and developing countries,

Stressing the need for effective international co-operation in the area of research, development and application of environmentally sound technologies,

Conscious of the crucial role of science and technology in the field of environmental protection and of the need of developing countries, in particular, concerning favourable access to environmentally sound technologies, processes, equipment and related research and expertise through international co-operation designed to further global efforts for environmental protection, including the use of innovative and effective means,

Recognizing that new and additional financial resources will have to be channelled to developing countries in order to ensure their full participation in global efforts for environmental protection,

1. *Decides* to convene a United Nations Conference on Environment and Development of two weeks' duration and at the highest possible level of participation to coincide with World Environment Day, 5 June, in 1992;

2. *Accepts with deep appreciation* the generous offer of the government of Brazil to host the Conference;

3. *Affirms* that the Conference should elaborate strategies and measures to halt and reverse the effects of environmental degradation in the context of strengthened national and international efforts to promote sustainable and environmentally sound development in all countries;

4. *Affirms* that the protection and enhancement of the environment are major issues that affect the well-being of peoples and economic development throughout the world;

5. *Also affirms* that the promotion of economic growth in developing countries is essential to address problems of environmental degradation;

6. *Further affirms* the importance of a supportive international economic environment that would result in sustained economic growth and development in all countries for protection and sound management of the environment;

7. *Reaffirms* that States have, in accordance with the Charter of the United Nations and the applicable principles of international law, the sovereign right to exploit their own resources pursuant to their environmental policies, and also reaffirms their responsibility to ensure that activities within their jurisdiction or control do not cause damage to the environment of other States or of areas beyond the limits of national jurisdiction and the need for States to play their due role in preserving and protecting the global and regional environment in accordance with their capacities and specific responsibilities;

8. *Affirms* the responsibility of States for the damage to the environment and natural resources caused by activities within their jurisdiction or control through transboundary interference, in accordance with national legislation and applicable international law;

9. *Notes* that the largest part of the current emission of pollutants into the environment, including toxic and hazardous wastes, originates in developed countries, and therefore recognizes that those countries have the main responsibility for combating such pollution;

10. *Stresses* that large industrial enterprises, including transnational corporations, are frequently the repositories of scarce technical skills for the

preservation and enhancement of the environment, conduct activities in sectors that have an impact on the environment and, to that extent, have specific responsibilities and that, in this context, efforts need to be encouraged and mobilized to protect and enhance the environment in all countries;

11. *Reaffirms* that the serious external indebtedness of developing countries, and other countries with serious debt-servicing problems, has to be addressed efficiently and urgently in order to enable those countries to contribute fully and in accordance with their capacities and responsibilities to global efforts to protect and enhance the environment;

12. *Affirms* that in the light of the above, the following environmental issues, which are not listed in any particular order of priority, are among those of major concern in maintaining the quality of the Earth's environment and especially in achieving environmentally sound and sustainable development in all countries:

a. Protection of the atmosphere by combating climate change, depletion of the ozone layer and transboundary air pollution;

b. Protection of the quality and supply of freshwater resources;

c. Protection of the oceans and all kinds of seas, including enclosed and semi-enclosed seas, and of coastal areas and the protection, rational use and development of their living resources;

d. Protection and management of land resources by, *inter alia*, combating deforestation, desertification and drought;

e. Conservation of biological diversity;

f. Environmentally sound management of biotechnology;

g. Environmentally sound management of wastes, particularly hazardous wastes, and of toxic chemicals, as well as prevention of illegal international traffic in toxic and dangerous products and wastes;

h. Improvement of the living and working environment of the poor in urban slums and rural areas, through eradicating poverty, *inter alia*, by implementing integrated rural and urban development programmes, as well as taking other appropriate measures at all levels necessary to stem the degradation of the environment;

i. Protection of human health conditions and improvement of the quality of life;

13. *Emphasizes* the need for strengthening international co-operation for the management of the environment to ensure its protection and enhancement and the need to explore the issue of benefits derived from activities, including research and development, related to the protection and development of biological diversity;

14. *Reaffirms* the need to strengthen international co-operation, particularly between developed and developing countries, in research and development and the utilization of environmentally sound technologies;

15. *Decides* that the Conference, in addressing environmental issues in the developmental context, should have the following objectives:

a. To examine the state of the environment and changes that have occurred since the 1972 United Nations Conference on the Human Environment and since the adoption of such international agreements as the Plan of Action to Combat Desertification,[165] the Vienna Convention for the Protection of the Ozone Layer, adopted on 22 March 1985, and the Montreal Protocol on Substances that Deplete the Ozone Layer, adopted on 16 September 1987, taking into account the actions taken by all countries and intergovernmental organizations to protect and enhance the environment;

b. To identify strategies to be co-ordinated regionally and globally, as appropriate, for concerted action to deal with major environmental issues in the socio-economic development processes of all countries within a particular time-frame;

c. To recommend measures to be taken at the national and international levels to protect and enhance the environment, taking into account the specific needs of developing countries, through the development and implementation of policies for sustainable and environmentally sound development with special emphasis on incorporating environmental concerns in the economic and social development process, and of various sectoral policies and through, *inter alia*, preventive action at the sources of environmental degradation, clearly identifying the sources of such degradation and appropriate remedial measures, in all countries;

d. To promote the further development of international environmental law, taking into account the Declaration of the United Nations Conference on Human Environment,[166] as well as the special needs and concerns of the developing countries, and to examine, in this context, the feasibility of elaborating general rights and obligations of States, as appropriate, in the field of the environment, also taking into account relevant existing international legal instruments;

e. To examine ways and means further to improve co-operation in the field of protection and enhancement of the environment between neighbouring countries with a view to eliminating adverse environmental effects;

f. To examine strategies for national and international action with a view to arriving at specific agreements and commitments by Governments for defined activities to deal with major environmental

165. *Report of the United Nations Conference on Desertification, Nairobi, 29 August–9 September 1977*(A/CONF.74/36), chap. 1.
166. See *Report of the United Nations Conference on the Human Environment* (United Nations publication, Sales No. E.73.11.A.14 and corrigendum).

issues, in order to restore the global ecological balance and to prevent further deterioration of the environment, taking into account the fact that the largest part of the current emission of pollutants into the environment, including toxic and hazardous wastes, originates in developed countries, and therefore recognizing that those countries have the main responsibility for combating such pollution;

g. To accord high priority to drought and desertification control and to consider all means necessary, including financial, scientific and technological resources, to halt and reverse the process of desertification with a view to preserving the ecological balance of the planet;

h. To examine the relationship between environmental degradation and the structure of the international economic environment, with a view to ensuring a more integrated approach to environment-and-development problems in relevant international forums without introducing new forms of conditionality;

i. To examine strategies for national and international action with a view to arriving at specific agreements and commitments by Governments and by intergovernmental organizations for defined activities to promote a supportive international economic environment that would result in sustained and environmentally sound development in all countries, with a view to combating poverty and improving the quality of life, and bearing in mind that the incorporation of environmental concerns and considerations in development planning and policies should not be used to introduce new forms of conditionality in aid or in development financing and should not serve as a pretext for creating unjustified barriers to trade;

j. To identify ways and means to provide new and additional financial resources, particularly to developing countries, for environmentally sound development programmes and projects in accordance with national development objectives, priorities and plans and to consider ways of establishing effective monitoring of the implementation of the provision of such new and additional financial resources, particularly to developing countries, so as to enable the international community to take further appropriate action on the basis of accurate and reliable data;

k. To identify ways and means to provide additional financial resources for measures directed towards solving major environmental problems of global concern and especially to support those countries, in particular developing countries, for whom the implementation of such measures would entail a special or abnormal burden, in particular owing to their lack of financial resources, expertise or technical capacity;

l. To consider various funding mechanisms, including voluntary ones, and to examine the possibility of a special international fund and other innovative approaches, with a view to ensuring the carrying out, on a favourable basis, of the most effective and expeditious transfer of environmentally sound technologies to developing countries;

m. To examine with the view to recommending effective modalities for favourable access to, and transfer of, environmentally sound technologies, in particular to the developing countries, including on concessional and preferential terms, and for supporting all countries in their efforts to create and develop their endogenous technological capacities in scientific research and development, as well as in the acquisition of relevant information, and, in this context, to explore the concept of assured access for developing countries to environmentally sound technologies in its relation to proprietary rights with a view to developing effective responses to the needs of developing countries in this area;

n. To promote the development of human resources, particularly in developing countries, for the protection and enhancement of the environment;

o. To recommend measures to Governments and the relevant bodies of the United Nations system, with a view to strengthening technical co-operation with the developing countries to enable them to develop and strengthen their capacity for identifying, analyzing, monitoring, managing or preventing environmental problems in accordance with their national development plans, objectives and priorities;

p. To promote open and timely exchange of information on national environmental policies, situations and accidents;

q. To review and examine the role of the United Nations system in dealing with the environment and possible ways of improving it;

r. To promote the development or strengthening of appropriate institutions at the national, regional and global levels to address environmental matters in the context of the socio-economic development processes of all countries;

s. To promote environmental education, especially of the younger generation, as well as other measures to increase awareness of the value of the environment;

t. To promote international co-operation within the United Nations system in monitoring, assessing and anticipating environmental threats and in rendering assistance in cases of environmental emergency;

u. To specify the respective responsibilities of and support to be given by the organs, organizations and programmes of the United Nations system for the implementation of the conclusion of the Conference;

v. To quantify the financial requirements for the successful implementation of Conference decisions and recommendations and to identify possible sources, including innovative ones, of additional resources;

w. To assess the capacity of the United Nations system to assist in the prevention and settlement of disputes in the environmental sphere and to recommend measures in this field, while respecting existing bilateral and international agreements that provide for the settlement of such disputes;

1. *Decides* to establish a Preparatory Committee of the General Assembly open to all States Members of the United Nations or members of the specialized agencies, with the participation of observers in accordance with the established practice of the General Assembly;

2. *Decides* that the Preparatory Committee shall hold an organizational session of two weeks' duration in March 1990 and a final session, both at United Nations Headquarters, in New York, and three additional substantive sessions, the first in Nairobi and the following two in Geneva, the timing and duration of which shall be determined by the Preparatory Committee at its organizational session;

3. *Decides* that the Preparatory Committee, at its organizational session, shall elect, with due regard to equitable geographic representation, the Chairman and other members of its bureau, comprising a substantial number of vice-chairmen and a rapporteur;

4. *Decides* that the host country of the Conference, Brazil, shall be *ex officio* a member of the Bureau;

5. *Requests* the Secretary-General of the United Nations, following the organizational session of the Preparatory Committee, to establish an appropriate *ad hoc* secretariat in Geneva, with a unit in New York and another unit in Nairobi, taking into account the decisions to be made by the Preparatory Committee regarding the preparatory process for the Conference and based on the principle of equitable geographic distribution;

6. *Decides* that the *ad hoc* secretariat will be headed by a Secretary-General of the Conference to be appointed by the Secretary-General of the United Nations;

7. *Requests* the Secretary-General of the United Nations to prepare a report for the organizational session of the Preparatory Committee containing recommendations on an adequate preparatory process, taking into account the provisions of the present resolution and the views expressed by Governments in the plenary debate at the forty-fourth session of the General Assembly;

8. *Decides* that the Preparatory Committee shall:

a. Draft the provisional agenda of the conference, in accordance with the provisions of the present resolution;

b. Adopt guidelines to enable States to take a harmonized approach in their preparations and reporting;

c. Prepare draft decisions for the Conference and submit them to the Conference for consideration and adoption;

9. *Requests* the United Nations Environment Programme, as the main organ for the environment, and requests the other organs, organizations and programmes of the United Nations system, as well as other relevant intergovernmental organizations, to contribute fully to the preparations of the Conference on the basis of guidelines and requirements to be established by the Preparatory Committee;

10. *Requests* the Secretary-General of the United Nations to ensure the co-ordination of contributions from the United Nations system, through the Administrative Committee on Co-ordination;

11. *Invites* all States to take an active part in the preparations for the Conference, to prepare national reports, as appropriate, to be submitted to the Preparatory Committee in a timely manner and to promote international co-operation and broad-based national preparatory processes involving the scientific community, industry, trade unions and concerned non-governmental organizations;

12. *Requests* relevant non-governmental organizations in consultative status with the Economic and Social Council to contribute to the Conference, as appropriate;

13. *Stresses* the importance of holding regional conferences on environment and development with the full co-operation of the regional commissions, and recommends that the results of such regional conferences be introduced into the preparatory process for the 1992 Conference, bearing in mind that regional conferences should make important substantive contributions to the Conference;

14. *Decides* that the preparatory process and the Conference itself should be funded through the regular budget of the United Nations without adversely affecting other, ongoing activities and without prejudice to the provision of sources of extrabudgetary resources;

15. *Decides* to establish a voluntary fund for the purpose of supporting developing countries, in particular the least developed among them, in participating fully and effectively in the Conference and in its preparatory process, and invites Governments to contribute to the fund;

16. *Requests* the chairman of the Preparatory Committee to report to the General Assembly at its forty-fifth and forty-sixth sessions on the progress of the work of the Committee;

17. *Decides* to include in the provisional agenda of its forty-fifth and forty-sixth sessions an item entitled "United Nations Conference on Environment and Development."

UN General Assembly Resolution on International Cooperation in the Field of Environment

44/229. Date: 22 December 1989   Meeting: 85
       Adopted without a vote   Report: A/44/746/Add.7 (as orally amended)

The General Assembly

Deeply concerned at the increasing degradation of the environment which, if allowed to continue, could endanger not only economic and social development but the very basis of life itself,

Noting the increased political interest in solving environmental problems and intensified international co-operation to that effect,

Welcoming that there have been encouraging developments in some important areas of environmental co-operation,

Reaffirming that there is a direct interrelationship between environment and development, and recognizing also that a favourable international economic environment that results in sustained economic growth and development, particularly in developing countries, is of major importance for sound management of the environment,

Reaffirming the importance of integrating environmental concerns and considerations into policies and programmes in all countries without introducing a new form of conditionality in aid or development financing or constituting a pretext for unjustified barriers to trade,

Noting the fact that the largest part of the current emission of pollutants into the environment, including toxic and hazardous wastes, originates in developed countries; and recognizing that those countries therefore have the main responsibility for combating such pollution,

Recognizing that serious environmental problems are arising for all countries and that those problems must be progressively addressed through preventive measures at their sources by national efforts and international co-operation,

Recalling decision 14/10 of the Governing Council of the United Nations Environment Programme on the environmental impact of *apartheid* on black agriculture in South Africa,[167]

Reaffirming also the need for developed countries and appropriate

---

167. See *Official Records of the General Assembly, Forty-third Session, Supplement, No. 25* (A/43/25), annex 1.

international organs and organizations to strengthen technical co-operation with developing countries, increase the transfer of technology and provide additional resources enhancing the capacity of developing countries to solve their environmental problems,

Recognizing that the United Nations Conference on Environment and Development in 1992 is a unique opportunity for all nations to address environmental and development issues in an integrated manner and to mobilize their political will to solve environmental problems through international co-operation,

Having considered the report of the Governing Council of the United Nations Environment Programme on the work of its fifteenth session,[168]

1. *Endorses* the work of the United Nations Environment Programme, welcomes the work on its fifteenth session[169] and takes note with appreciation of its decisions, as adopted, in light of this resolution;

2. *Reaffirms* the mandate of the United Nations Environment Programme as defined in General Assembly resolution 2997 (XXVII) and supports further strengthening of the role of the Environment Programme as the central catalyzing, co-ordinating and stimulating body in the field of the environment within the United Nations system;

3. *Welcomes* the steps taken by the Governing Council of the United Nations Environment Programme to improve its own effectiveness and efficiency in its decision 15/1 of 25 May 1989;

4. *Reaffirms* that the United Nations system, through the General Assembly, due to its universal character, is the appropriate forum for concerted political action on global environmental problems;

5. *Considers* in this regard that the structure and responsiveness of the United Nations to deal with major environmental issues should be reviewed in order to strengthen its capacity in dealing with these matters in an integrated, coherent and effective way and requests the Secretary-General to prepare a report on this issue taking into account the views expressed by Governments, to be considered in the preparatory process of the United Nations Conference on Environment and Development;

6. *Takes note* of the areas of concentration for the international community set out by the Governing Council in its decision 15/1, section IV, and with the list of issues within those areas which are not listed in any particular order of priority to which the United Nations Environment Programme should give special attention;

7. *Takes note* of the Governing Council decision 15/4 of 26 May 1989

---

168. See *Official Records of the General Assembly, Forty-fourth Session, Supplement No. 25* (A/44/25), annex 1.
169. Ibid.

and supports its decision to hold a special session in 1990 of three days' duration at the same location, and in conjunction with the first substantive session of the Preparatory Committee of the United Nations Conference on Environment and Development, which, at its organizational session, should bear this issue in mind with a view to achieving an effective preparatory process for the Conference. This special session should deal with the elaboration of, and the process of making and implementing decisions on, priority environmental issues, in particular ways and means of enhancing the role of the United Nations Environment Programme within the United Nations system in addressing those issues;

8. *Reaffirms* the need to provide new and additional financial resources to support developing countries in identifying, analyzing, monitoring, preventing and managing environmental problems primarily at their source, in accordance with their national development goals, objectives and plans, so as to ensure that their development priorities are not adversely affected;

9. *Stresses* the need for new and additional financial resources for measures towards solving major environmental problems of global concern, and especially to support those countries, in particular developing countries for whom the implementation of such measures would entail a special or abnormal burden, in particular due to their lack of financial resources, expertise and/or technical capacity;

10. *Expresses its appreciation* at indications that the flow of resources to the United Nations Environment Fund is increasing in real terms, and endorses the annual target of a minimum of one hundred million United States dollars in contributions by the year 1992, taking into account the increasing tasks of the United Nations Environment Programme, and calls upon all Governments to contribute or increase their contributions to the Fund by at least 35 percent per annum from the 1 January 1989 level to enable that target to be met by 1992;

11. *Endorses* the views and suggestions of the Governing Council of the United Nations Environment Programme as expressed in its decision 15/2 on the implementation of resolutions 42/186 and 42/187 of 11 December 1987 as a positive step towards a better understanding of the concept of sustainable and environmentally sound development by all countries;

12. *Takes note* of the recommendation made by the Governing Council of the United Nations Environment Programme in its decision 15/5 of 25 May 1989 and stresses that sustainable and environmentally sound development in all countries should become one of the central guiding principles in the international development strategy being elaborated for the fourth United Nations development decade;

13. *Concurs* with Governing Council decision 15/14 of 25 May 1989 on the clearing-house function, in which it is proposed that the United Nations Environment Programme should play a more vigorous role in

supporting developing countries, upon their request, in the following undertakings:

  a. To establish and strengthen their institutions and professional capacities to integrate environmental considerations into their development policies and planning;

  b. To formulate and initiate programmes and activities for dealing with their most serious environmental problems;

  c. To formulate and participate in action plans for the common management of ecosystems and critical environmental problems at the national, regional and global levels;

  14. *Stresses* that sustainable and environmentally sound development requires changes in the unsustainable pattern of production and consumption, particularly in industrialized countries, and the development of environmentally sound technologies, and, in this context, stresses also the need to examine with a view to recommend effective modalities for favourable access to, and transfer of, environmentally sound technologies, in particular to the developing countries, including on concessional and preferential terms, and for supporting all countries in their efforts to create and develop their endogenous technological capacities in the field of scientific research and development as well as in the acquisition of relevant information and, in this context, to explore the concept of assured access, for developing countries, to environmentally sound technologies, in its relation to proprietary rights, with a view to developing effective responses to the needs of developing countries in this area;

  15. *Takes note* of the decision 15/24 of 25 May 1989 of the Governing Council on sustainable agriculture and calls upon the Governing Council to pay special attention to its implementation;

  16. *Reaffirms* the urgent need for Governments, multilateral organizations and government and non-governmental financial institutions to take into account in their policies, decision-making processes and financial mechanisms the relationship between the foreign debt and the ability of developing countries to strengthen their capacity to address the critical environmental issues fundamental to development and protection of the environment;

  17. *Urges* the Intergovernmental Panel on Climate Change to take the necessary steps to ensure the scientific and policy participation of developing countries in its work, and calls upon the international community, in particular the developed countries, to consider contributing generously to the Intergovernmental Panel on Climate Change trust fund with a view to financing the participation of experts designated by Governments of the developing countries in all the meetings of the Panel including its working groups and sub-groups;

  18. *Supports* the request made by the Governing Council of the United

Nations Environment Programme, in its decision 15/36, that the Executive Director of the Programme, in co-operation with the Secretary-General of the World Meteorological Organization, begin preparations for negotiations on a framework convention on climate, taking into account the work on the Intergovernmental Panel on Climate Change and its interim report, as well as the results achieved at international meetings on the subject, including the Second World Climate Conference, and recommends that such negotiations begin as soon as possible after the adoption of the interim report of the Intergovernmental Panel on Climate Change and that the General Assembly at an early date during its forty-fifth session take a decision recommending ways and means and modalities for further pursuing these negotiations, taking into account the work of the Preparatory Committee for the 1992 Conference on Environment and Development;

19. *Notes with satisfaction* the progress made on the protection of the ozone layer and urges all States to co-operate with the Executive Director of the United Nations Environment Programme in the process of strengthening the Montreal Protocol on Substances that Deplete the Ozone Layer in the light of the Helsinki Declaration on the Protection of the Ozone Layer of 2 May 1989,[170] emphasizes the importance of taking into account the special needs and requirements of developing countries and developing appropriate funding mechanisms in order to enable all, and, in particular, developing countries, to participate effectively in the revised protocol;

20. *Notes further* the adoption, on 22 March 1989, of the Basel Convention on the Control of Transboundary Movements of Hazardous Wastes and their Disposal,[171] and calls upon all States to consider signing the Basel Convention without prejudice to the final position to be adopted by regional organizations in this regard and to strengthen their co-operation in problem areas within the scope of the Convention;

21. *Supports* Governing Council decision 15/23 of 25 May 1989 on drought and desertification in which the Council, *inter alia*, invites donor Governments and intergovernmental bodies to accord high priority in their bilateral and multilateral assistance to national programmes for combating desertification and for the rehabilitation of land resources;

22. *Considers* the conservation and utilization of biological diversity to be a priority issue, an important element of ecological balance and as a source of benefit to mankind and welcomes decision 15/34 of 25 May 1989 of the Governing Council of the United Nations Environment Programme;

23. *Notes* the consideration given by the Governing Council in its decision 15/10 of 25 May 1989 to the proposed establishment of a United Nations center for urgent environmental assistance and further notes the

170. *See* UNEP/Ozl. Pro. 1/5, appendix I.
171. *See* UNEP/IG.80/3.

information provided by the Executive Director of the United Nations
Environment Programme on the preliminary results of his consultations
regarding the views expressed by Governments and organizations on this
matter bearing in mind the mandate of the United Nations Environment
Programme, the Office of the United Nations Disaster Relief Co-ordinator,
the World Meteorological Organization, the International Maritime
Organization and the International Atomic Energy Agency as well as other
relevant United Nations specialized agencies and bodies;

24. *Expresses its satisfaction* at the impetus given to addressing
environmental concerns through meetings at the regional level and calls on
the United Nations Environment Programme and other relevant organizations
to continue to play an effective role in this regard.

About the Authors

LUIS ALVARADO is Minister of National Assets and President of the National Commission on the Environment, Chile.

JOSÉ LUTZENBERGER is Secretary for the Environment, Presidency of the Republic, Brazil.

HERALDO MUÑOZ is Ambassador of Chile to the Organization of American States and President of the Committee on the Environment of the OAS.

JOAO BAENA SOARES is Career Ambassador of the Foreign Service of Brazil and Secretary General of the Organization of American States (OAS).

MOSTAFA K. TOLBA is Executive Director, United Nations Environment Programme (UNEP).